Deism and Social Ethics
the role of religion in the third millennium

Robert Corfe is a prolific author who has written extensively on the benefits of social capitalism. He is a political scientist and businessman, with considerable experience of political life, and in this book he argues the need for a regenerated deism in helping secure a safer and more peaceful world in diminishing religiously-motivated political strife. For many years he was a senior manager in manufacturing industry, and later a management consultant advising SMEs, usually in the engineering sector. He is also the author of two autobiographical books under different pseudonyms: *Death in Riyadh dark secrets in hidden Arabia* (Geoff Carter), based on his experiences as a businessman in the Middle East in the 1980s, and, *My Conflict With A Soviet Spy the story of the Ron Evans spy case* (Eddie Miller), based on his adventures in Scandinavia in the 1960s. In 1987 he founded the Campaign For Industry, to which he was elected Chairman, and for which he wrote many pamphlets on the problems of contemporary business. His broad experience, frequent travels overseas, and years of residence in Continental Europe have given him a unique perspective of socio-economic issues.

By the same author –

Freedom From America
*for safeguarding democracy & the economic & cultural integrity of
peoples*

Populism Against Progress
and the collapse of aspirational values

Forthcoming –

Egalitarianism of the Free Society
and the end of class conflict

Social Capitalism in theory and practice

Vol. 1
Emergence of the New Majority

Vol. 2
The People's Capitalism

Vol. 3
Prosperity in a stable World

Deism and Social Ethics

the role of religion in the third millennium

Robert Corfe

Arena Books

First published in 2007 by Arena Books

Arena Books
6 Southgate Green
Bury St. Edmunds
IP33 2BL

www.arenabooks.co.uk

Corfe, Robert
    Deism and Social Ethics the role of religion in the third millennium
    1. Deism 2. Religion and sociology 3. Social ethics
    I. Title
    211.5

ISBN-13 978-0-9543161-9-8

BIC classifications:- HRAM 1 & 2 (v1. HRLB3 & HRAN)

Printed and bound by Lightning Source UK

Cover design
By Jon Baxter

Typeset in
Times New Roman

PREFACE

The role of Deism in the contemporary world

It would have been surprising to people in the industrialised economies, of only a generation ago, if the prediction had been made that the world would one day be witness to the resurgence of religious fanaticism as the most troubling factor in international politics. They would have scoffed at such a prediction as absurd and incredible, in defying the natural beneficence of technological progress.

And yet now we find ourselves at the start of the 21st century, in a world of religious tension and conflict – worsening year by year – on a scale not witnessed since the 17th century. But whilst in the 17th century that conflict was confined to Europe, and to the divisions of Christianity, today it is global, and divides nations both within and externally, including those of cultural, racial, and language groups. Fundamentalism, both Christian and Islamic, gives rise to the greatest conflictual ills disturbing the peace of our planet, but these have been followed by the rise of Hindu fundamentalism, and smaller but equally vicious divides in the Balkans and elsewhere.

The sociological significance of religious conflict is still not properly understood or taken with the seriousness it deserves by academics in the industrialised West. It is either given a Marxist interpretation in terms of underlying economic causes, and such interpretations are unhelpful, and anyway, misleading; or else religion is dismissed as the outcome of the superstitions of the past which the world is at fault for being too slow to outgrow. Again, this is a simplistic attitude which fails to reflect the reality of the human condition and its true complexity.

Researchers and academia, throughout the advanced industrialised world, in both the West and the Far East, are predominantly agnostic or atheistic in temperament, and for that they cannot be blamed. The first duty of their profession is loyalty to the factual or demonstrable truth, and any religion based on revelation (which is most) defies the truth in terms of rationalism and science. Most educated people are agnostic, but have sufficient sensibility in avoiding offence to those with religious belief. Hence religion has not only become a taboo topic in polite society, but in scholarly circles, is ignored as a hot potato best left alone.

When, however, on the rare occasion, an academic does emerge to discuss the issue of religion, it is almost invariably to present an uncompromising atheism as the only path to proper thinking on the unknowable. And the atheistic arguments are simple and have been repeated over the centuries, with occasional refinements in deferring to the latest discoveries of science. This, in turn, strengthens the general agnosticism throughout society, whilst still leaving the churches untouched to continue their work as before – except with declining congregations. This is the natural response of a polite society in a free world.

The facile arguments of atheism have never needed to be more than slender, but that great thinker who modernised our view of science, Sir Francis Bacon, correctly observed that, "It is true that a little philosophy inclineth man's mind to atheism; but depth in philosophy bringeth men's minds about to religion; for while the mind of man looketh upon second causes scattered, it may sometimes rest in them, and go no further; but when it beholdeth the chain of them, confederate and linked together it must needs fly to Providence and Deity."[1] And this reflects the underlying nature of humankind, and helps explain the tenacity of religion as a social fact.

Predictions on the demise of religion are to be found on an unending horizon. The predictions have been too many and too confident for too long, and always based on "sound factual evidence" which seems to come to nought. Of course there are upward and downward swings, but always, unexpectedly, religion seems to bounce back just when its extinction was foretold. Religion has always existed, in one form or another, sometimes for good and sometimes for ill, and it is likely to survive as long as the human race. The reason, as explained in

---

[1] In his Essay, *Of Atheism.*

this book, is that religion is an essential component of humankind. Men and women are by nature spiritual beings in that they cherish hopes and aspirations which are neither satisfied by material comforts or security, nor by the enlightenment or evidence of scientific discovery. Hence religion is as much a component of human nature as the physical components of our bodies.

The issues which would seem to contradict such a contention are the failures within religion itself. Religion needs to evolve with the general evolution of society – and indeed, has evolved through its long history over the millennia. But the major world religions have not evolved over the past few hundred years – or at least, they have not evolved sufficiently in keeping apace with progress. The Christian churches have indulged in a lot of patchwork in covering up tears or worn parts, but it has done little in either improving their appearance or in strengthening their credibility.

Whilst in Europe Christianity survives predominantly as a living death, respected as an ancient institution but little more; in America and elsewhere, duplicitous evangelising exploits the ignorant, and has given rise to fundamentalist churches with social and political consequences of real evil. Neither extensive patchwork nor clever marketing is sufficient to revive an ailing Christianity, for the obvious reason that both such approaches contradict the need for openness and truth, so essential for the purity of religion. It may be that Christianity is impervious to the kind of changes necessary, and if this is the case, then theologians are faced with a bleak task ahead.

But the greatest problem of religion today does not arise from its internal failures, but from irreconcilable differences between different faiths and the consequential bloodshed and terrorism of political conflict. There is no real compromise or dialogue between Islam and Christianity, because each is ruled by its dogma and distinctive viewpoints of the world. The clash of fundamentalisms arises from *irrationalism* alone, and the resulting dehumanising of thought on the most important issues to humankind. But the bloodiest religious divide at the present time, it should be noted, in terms of actual lives lost, is not between Christians and Moslems, but between the Sunni and Shia sects of the latter faith.

Religious faiths which mutate into political movements have always expressed extreme intolerance. The authority of their Godhead forbids them from seeing the world in any other light than that of the "truth" faith. They act not according to reason or commonsense, but according to the prescriptive rules of "divine" authority, and this restricts their range for free thought or intelligent discretion. Furthermore, they tend to act on inspiration rather than through consultation. Thus George W. Bush responds directly to the commands of "God" with regard to implementing a policy towards Iraq, to no lesser degree than Osama bin Laden decides to bomb the World Trade Centre. These policies are decided in cultural environments very different from one another, but the psychological environments are the same.

This is what makes religion so very dangerous at the present time. Everyone on our planet lives under an identical threat. Political power which is at odds with reason makes for a very unpredictable future, and where the impossible is made possible. Those who are ruled by religion through revelation inescapably have a weakened concern for the issues of the terrestrial world, for the simple reason that they are constantly reminded that this life is merely a preparation for a better future. People who live under such a misconception, even if they only half believe it, are far more prepared to take greater risks – especially with other peoples' lives – than those who are more sceptical about the afterlife.

And so, too, those at the base of the population who look forward to a celestial existence, are far more willing to obey their masters and sacrifice their lives for a "great cause," than the agnostic majority. It would be interesting to speculate how many amongst the 9/11 terrorists would have refrained from their venture if it was not for the promise of enjoying fifty-seven virgins in their next and better life. Warfare, of course, has always been a good thing for the Church, for then the clergy are always assured of fuller congregations than before.

Religion in the guise of politics – or vice versa, for they are both the same – is always ruthless. The horror which faces us today, is not that politics or outrages in its name are pursued by tiny minorities, for this has always been the case, but that the knowledge and resources for mass destruction are at the disposal of anyone with internet access and initiative somewhat above the average. Those with sufficient capital for worldwide travel, and passports for entry into any state, and bribes for purchasing nuclear explosives or a dirty bomb, may precipitate the most horrific acts in the name of God. Underground railway systems may be blown up; atomic power stations may be sabotaged and millions around irradiated as a consequence; crowds may be bombed in any location, in markets, clubs, or churches; or entire cities may be blasted into extinction.

These threats and the tensions stemming from them are exacerbated by the response they incur. Those who view the world in dualistic terms, i.e. the adherents of the three Abrahamic religions, instinctively cry that Good shall confront Evil, that Might shall confront Cowardice, and that Light shall triumph over Darkness. None of this emotional self-righteousness begins to resolve real problems, for it amounts to little more than the crude reiteration that, "I am right and you are wrong and there's nothing more to be said."

This is the international situation as we find it today, and the sane majority are made to feel that their future rests in the hands of a few quarrelling religious bigots. What is the way out of this impenetrable situation? Firstly, there is the need for the intercession of something which transcends the petty viewpoint of party or national politics. Secondly, and more significantly, there is the need for a communication link fitting the demands of the religious instinct whilst also insisting on the authority of God. How are such things to be intellectualised for a practical purpose? When power is brought under the authority of religion, then only religious means are likely to break the deadlock when differences emerge.

Only through regenerating the ethical power of deism can there be hope for breaking through the stubbornness and obscurantism which exists today. A regenerated deism has the potential to work as a religious influence transcending all churches and sects. This is because it is based in rationalism and a scientific ethics for humankind and the cosmos, which dispenses with revelation, and repudiates the myths and mysteries of organised religion. It upholds the belief in God as an essence, or coming into being of the Good, and concurs with the spirit and fact of evolutionary development, and the conclusions of contemporary science.

Deism is a religion for the peoples of the third millennium, for it rejects the falsehood of the past and embraces the eternal truths of ethical life. It meets the spirit and challenges of the age, and in its toleration, attracts the commitment of the intelligent and healthy sceptical in all walks of life. Because of its minimalist theology, it is an over-arching religion, able to act as a bridge between the organised churches and the non-believer, or as a natural communication link between faiths in conflict.

Because deism is above party politics, or national or factional interests, and because it is committed to searching for ultimate ethical truths, it has always been concerned with this-worldly as opposed to other-worldly concerns since the time of Cromwell. As will be shown later in this book, Cromwell hated the deists, for he was unable to manipulate them by exploiting the possibility of religious zeal in using them for his own political purposes. So likewise, today, the potential value of deism in the sphere of politics is to stand apart from the storm and stress of conflict arising from common misunderstanding or superstition, and to analyse sociological realities before attempting the role of peacemaker.

Hence deism offers a new perspective of the ills of the world and a fresh approach to resolving its conflicts. Deists have never been formed into an organised movement, but operate in independent groups or as individuals maintaining friendly contacts, and an exchange of views through papers and journals across the globe. The great age of English deism was the first half of the 18th century, from where it spread with renewed vigour throughout the Continent, and then with great effect to the American colonies. After that great flowering more than two hundred years ago, deism declined rapidly and sank into insignificance.

The purpose of the present book is to regenerate a new deism to suit the needs of the 21st century. Up until the present time, Thomas Paine's the, *Age of Reason*, is still cited as the leading deist text, although it was not written and published until almost four decades after the close of the great epoch of English deism. In this book an attempt is made to present an updated philosophical-theology for deism in broadening its appeal, as well as repudiating some of the absurdities which have surrounded the deism of the past.

The tendency in the past was to openly deny the idea of *faith* in favour of reason. We have chosen to re-define faith in returning it to its proper meaning as, "complete trust or confidence."[2] This is usually the first of some five or so definitions given in the most authoritative dictionaries. Hence, I have faith that two and two make four, or that dawn will follow night. Another definition is "fidelity; adherence to duty or engagements; constancy."[3] No deist would question these definitions.

The concept of God which we have presented in the second chapter is irrefutable, and does not attempt to exploit the credulity of those of the lowest or highest intelligence, or to stretch the imagination of the dullest intellect. It entails no more than the ever-present potential of the coming-into-being of the good, and is demonstrated through evolution and natural selection, and through the progress of society towards a better and more ethical life. God is perceived as a purely ethical essence in the universe, and is in no sense a conscious decision-making being to be called-upon at our will. Of course there are conditional factors in refining such a definition which are

---

[2] *Oxford Encyclopedic Dictionary*, OUP, 1991, p. 508.
[3] *Lloyd's Encyclopædic Dictionary*, 1895, Vol III, p. 463.

considered in the text. This, then, is a God in which we can have *absolute faith* because he is immanent in the working of the physical universe and the idea of his existence which has sprung from it.

Only a religion which can demonstrate its freedom from falsehood can hope to capture the imagination of intelligent people of goodwill in the 21st century. This is because rational people, motivated by a moral purpose, who seek to resolve problems in their own mind and then apply them on a practical basis, are too often filled with repugnance by what they see as the intellectual deceit of theological arguments; the circumlocutionary explanations for impossible or so-called "miraculous" events; the psychological trickery used in arousing collective zeal for commitment to the faith; and most of all, the call to believe in a God who *wills* unspeakable evils in the world of his creation. All such arguments are too reminiscent of the insurance or double-glazing salesman's knock on the door. And besides, such theologising is too far removed from our own sense of sound reality, and what we feel should constitute the truth.

How should deists apply their teaching in the world as we find it? Crowd-pulling is not the deist's style, and neither would they feel comfortable in implementing such methods, although seminars and discussion groups would always be welcome in expanding the horizon of their understanding. As reasonable people, deists are calm and often self-effacing, but always seeking to extend their knowledge. Because we live in a world of constant change they are necessarily tolerant and averse to dogma, and what our 18th century forebears described as the vice of "enthusiasm."

Deists should quietly apply their teaching on two levels. Firstly, agnostics or unbelievers may be openly proselytised in supporting the deist cause as potential front-line propagandists of the deist philosophy – for deism is more strictly a philosophy than a theology. Secondly, those belonging to organised churches or sects should be approached with the greatest circumspection. Deism should never seek to offend, although in the name of truth, much deist writing will inevitably provoke those committed to church dogma.

Deists may join and participate in the various churches of their choice, but not for the purpose of overt proselytising, but rather to merely inform or teach the principles of deism. Attempts should not be made to draw Anglicans, Roman Catholics, or Islamists, etc., away from their traditional faiths, but rather to turn their mindset towards deistic modes of thought, whilst still retaining existing loyalties. In this way deism will achieve greater influence worldwide through ideas which eventually penetrate the various churches themselves.

The ultimate aim of deism in this sphere of activity, is not to destroy or harm the organised churches, but rather to change them, and bring them towards a closer feeling of unity and identity. Deism is above all an ethical movement, and an ethics not based on the commands of some religious leader, but on an objective or scientific consideration of factors concerned with the longer term needs of humankind and the planet on which we live. It is through goodwill and the disinterested search for truth that deists should seek to win the trust and respect of all religious leaders.

And neither should deists undervalue the good work of the existing churches. Many church leaders today have an intelligence and imaginative grasp of political issues for justice and equity which often puts our shoddy parliamentary representatives in the shade. The clergyman is especially well placed as a valued contributor to political debate, since he is not a "party" man or woman, and so may adopt a more disinterested viewpoint. The Anglican clergy, as also the Lutherans of Germany and Scandinavia, take a thoughtful and benign view of world affairs, and the two thousand year history of Roman Catholicism has given that church a realistic and sympathetic understanding of human nature.

Meanwhile, on the other side of the spectrum, the Unitarians and Quakers have always been a force for good, and Quaker business has not only traditionally been highly successful in finance and manufacturing, but promoted ethical capitalist practices, through the sufficient re-investment of profits in sustaining industry for the longer term. Other free churches, on the contrary, as we show in this book, have been the source of social evil on a widespread scale, either through promoting hatred of those different from themselves; or demonstrating their limited understanding of the human psyche; or promoting ignorance, or putting ignorance on a pedestal; or generating a fanaticism which is harmful to the personality in several ways.

The task of deists in seeking the good of the world is unlimited. This is because they may be found in all walks of life, and hopefully, in the not-too-distant future, as the leaders of nation states seeking the peace of the world. As practical people, they should not avoid the messy and often corrupting career of party politics, but rather meet that challenge through their spiritual strength as deists. Deism has always been democratic and a religion of this world and should remain so, and the deists who confronted the dictatorial power of Cromwell should remain an inspiration for the future.

Those deists working on a more modest level, amongst the ordinary population, have a task which collectively, is no less significant in the struggle for a more secure and better world in the millennium ahead. A world which for the longer term is free of strife, widespread crime, and war, is not to be achieved by the cynical pragmatism of statesmen bargaining the interests of one sector of the population against another, as we have seen for too long in the past century, but through arousing the consciousness of social ethics amongst all humanity. Only then, when those at the base of society, achieve the forethought and moral awareness to hold their leaders to account, will the latter be obliged to maintain the justice and equity of the good society.

Robert Corfe
June 2007

CONTENTS

CONTENTS

CONTENTS

CONTENTS

CHAPTER 10
How Ethics Relies on Truth

CHAPTER 11
The Problem of Sexual Morality

CHAPTER 1

THE CRISIS OF RELIGION IN THE MODERN WORLD

"A man's 'religion' consists not of the many things he is in
doubt of and tries to believe, but of the few he is assured of,
and has no need of effort believing."

Thomas Carlyle, *Latter-Day Pamphlets*, No. 8, 1850.

1 – The tenacity of religion

Religion is intrinsic to the nature of humankind. In all
ages and in all cultures it is always manifested in one
form or another, sometimes as a beneficent influence
and sometimes as a malevolent force, but always it has emerged
within the consciousness of society, sometimes with the
violence of fanaticism and sometimes as a weak brew pushed to
the margins of existence.

In the Western world, over the past few centuries, its
demise has often been foretold, but just when it seemed on the
verge of extinction under the wave of scientific discovery or the
surge of materialism, it has always revived with strength and
zeal to surprise leading opinion-formers. Agnostic and even
atheistic thinkers have flourished from ancient times until the
present, and they have presented their ideas with clarity and
force, and the same arguments with occasional refinements,
have been presented from one epoch to another, but they have
seldom if ever exerted significant influence in changing the
entrenched religious perceptions of the majority.

None of this should be construed as an apology for the
beliefs or practices of religion at particular periods of history,
for militant agnostic and atheistic thinkers have often rendered
valuable service to humanity in attacking the abuses and
injustices arising from religion. But it has nonetheless
demonstrated clearly, from the earliest times until the present,
the tenacity of religion and the futility of atheism in attempting
to replace it on the throne of authority. Most surprising in recent

history was to witness the resurgence of the Orthodox Church in the former Soviet Union after the collapse of Communism. Surely 70 years of atheistic indoctrination, as one generation followed another, should have left its permanent mark in changing the mentality of a people! But no, the Church seemed to regain its status and its splendour as if no interregnum had divided the present from the time of the Tsars.

2 – A natural component of human nature

Religion has much which seems to defy the progress of science and modernity, as well as commonsense and rationality, but it nonetheless survives as a living reality. What is it in the human psyche which ensures the survival of the religious spirit – for it is certainly not the organisation of religion by priests and theologians which maintains its existence? Religion is predominantly a spontaneous process, springing from the base of the population, from diffused groups and the inspiration of leaders who seemingly emerge from nowhere, than a phenomenon imposed from above. The post-Reformation period, and especially in the New World in the 20th century have amply demonstrated these facts.

There are two factors which seem to ensure the survival of religion, and at the same time establish that it forms a natural and irreplaceable part of the human psyche. The first stems from an underlying ethical sense in that all striving for success and development, and the universe and the nature of existence is based in an unknown moral order, and that the fear and warding off of difficulties and evil calls for the propitiation of hidden forces. An awareness of these factors generates a sense of awe in the face of fate and the unpredictability of what lies ahead. And from this emerges a deferential attitude to the world and what lies beyond it, and a sense of care, and an ethical view on life and on major decision-making.

These characteristics are common to all religions, from the Homoeopathic magic of the primitive tribe to the monotheistic beliefs as they are practised at the present day. Whilst religions may be manifested in a thousand and one variations, it should be noted that they all spring from the human emotions of Hope, Uncertainty, and Fear, and that these eternal attributes of the human condition do not change from one millennium to another. Hence, whilst the imagination is used to construct complex theologies; elaborate rituals, often with dance and song; great cathedrals; inimitable masterworks of art; and powerful bureaucracies under a hierarchy of priests, all these things are motivated by three basic human emotions.

3 – The fear of destiny

Whilst the first factor in ensuring the survival of religion is seen from the perspective of Social life, the second is seen from the Personal. There comes a point in the lives of most people – sometimes at frequent intervals – when they are confronted by problems which are seemingly unresolvable through their own efforts. This is when knowledge, skill, or willpower, is all of no avail. They become victims of fate which exerts the ultimate authority. Up until the start of the 20th century, with the advance of science and modern medical practice, people were placed in the hands of fate on serious life issues far more frequently than they are today. If average life expectancy was between 35-40 this was only because disease took away so large a part of the population.

If families had 8-10 children, this was not because their parents had such a great love for offspring, but because they wanted to ensure that at least several would reach adulthood, and that they in their turn should have children. In such a society there were strong motivations for religion to flourish, for the helpless parent (irrespective of his or her social status) was in the hands of fate with regard to a sick infant. When typhus or cholera struck, the doctor's medical aid was of little help, and his mere diagnosis was hardly less than a death sentence. Kind words were often his only consolation, and the rest depended on the prayers of relatives and friends.

Even today in the 21st century fate exerts its power in many life-threatening situations. Apart from the ravages of war and famine and disease in overseas locations, there are road and rail accidents; Tsunami and hurricane disasters; the aftermath of earthquakes and volcanic irruptions; the fear of meteorites from outer space plunging into our planet; and most recently, the prospect of climate change, and the flooding of vast areas of agricultural land and heavily populated cities. In addition to these threats no individual can predict what tomorrow will bring. Death may always be around the corner. The visit of the grim reaper is always unpredictable and unknown.

As a child during the Second World War, I well remember the desperate anxiety of my paternal grandmother over the fate of her younger sons on active service abroad. Her youngest, and perhaps her favourite son, was in the Tank Corps in North Africa and later in Italy, encountering battle situations, whilst my other uncle was in the RAF, also in North Africa – although he wrote home reassuringly that he spent most his time lying lazily in the shade of banana trees.

My grandmother, nonetheless, reminded us on frequent occasions that she prayed, not only at bedtime, but all day long from the moment she awoke, for the safety of her sons, and on more than one occasion, she spoke about the Angel of Mons and God's miracle enabling the British advance against the hated Germans – albeit for a mere few hundred yards, and for a temporary period – in the first World War. She was, of course, placed in exactly the same situation as millions of other mothers in Europe and throughout the world at that time, but could anyone have dared, or been so insensitive as to reproach her for her religiosity? What power had she to influence events or to safeguard her sons? Prayer was the only psychological outlet which remained.

4 – Anxiety is no moral justification for religion

In the face of all these factors there are hardly fewer reasons for religion to flourish today than in yesteryear. But it should be noted that none of the factors cited above are a justification for the existence or perpetuation of religion. They are no more than an *explanation* for the presence of religion.

This is because ceremonies, rituals, or petitionary formularies, with the end purpose of obtaining a desired response from a supreme being, are no more moral in themselves than the practical application of a car mechanic in repairing a broken down vehicle. The only difference between the two is that whilst the religious supplicant is motivated by the unconscious influence of psychological stress, the mechanic is influenced by his rational application in resolving an immediate problem. As we shall demonstrate throughout this book, the only justification for modern religion in the advanced and educated industrialised world is when it is motivated solely by a disinterested higher ethical purpose.

Despite our affirmation that religion is natural to humankind, and cannot be extirpated by the state, or the spread of humanism, or by any other means, now in the 21st century, there is no cause for complacency, for the future of organised religion as a healthy or beneficial influence in the years which lied ahead.

It is not so much the churches which today are in worldwide crisis, as religion itself, and the following chapters are concerned with the core values of religion as understood from their ethical aspect.

5 – The crisis of contemporary religion

The crisis of religion has been brought about by scientific and technological changes over the past 400 years, although for the greater part of that period, the churches have been protected by the wall of tradition and popular sentiment. And now that protection is falling away, like ice exposed to the sun, and in the West at any rate, Christianity is now withering at a speed which it never did when faced by the materialistic movements of the 19th century. Whilst the Roman Catholic church is facing the possibility of losing up to a quarter of its priests due to the desire to forego a celibate life in favour of marriage, the pews of the Protestant churches become more empty with every passing Sunday.

Whilst the crisis of the Anglican church is exacerbated by its conservatism, and acrimonious disputes on women clergy and the sexual orientation of its male clergy; the Lutheran and Reformed churches on the Continent are brought into disrepute by a striking modernism and break with the past, which seems to deprive them of their remaining remnants of spirituality. Meanwhile, the Decade of Evangelism, launched with such high hopes back in 1992, fell into tatters within a year, and was soon dismissed with scorn by leading churchmen from many parts of the country. What was intended to be a crusade of light was darkened by the offence it caused in so many quarters.

The Decade of Evangelism was a hurried and ill thought out project. It seemed not to have appreciated that we are now living in a multi-cultural society. Not only did the Jews for Jesus campaign arouse fury amongst our Jewish brethren, but even more significantly, it came up against the far greater number of Islamic faithful now living in our midst. The latter have responded by turning inwards to their own brand of fundamentalism, and even by an attempt to form an Islamic parliament as an alternative to the established institutions of Westminster.

If these problems of religion are seen on the national scale, as merely those of Britain, they also have a worldwide resonance of equal intensity. It is not necessary to extend one's vision as far as the Caucasus, where the break-up of the Soviet Union is now exposing a huge potential clash between a variety of Christian and Muslim peoples living cheek by jowl; for here on our own doorstep, in France and Germany, mounting tensions are experienced between religious groups with widely differing cultural backgrounds – not to mention the conflict between Catholics and Protestants in Ulster. Whilst Berlin has now the second largest Turkish Muslim population of any city in the world, there are now entire districts of Paris and Marseilles that today are more African than European in character. Most recently, French legislation against certain religious sects in safeguarding the integrity of the individual personality, has given rise to considerable controversy – not to mention legislation affecting the Islamic population with regard to banning the wearing of headscarves in school. Meanwhile, the clash between Jew and Arab in the Middle East, is not only the most long-lasting but remains the most explosive of these religious conflicts. The consequence of these different mixes is racism and neo-fascism.

What should be the response of the churches to this situation? It cannot, as in centuries past, be the response of violence. What, then, is the alternative? It can only be by searching out the truth – and this may be painful and difficult – but no other alternative is open. It is necessary to turn to the core values of religion – not to any specific religion – but to religion in the abstract. For this purpose, all doctrines and beliefs founded on myth, must first be put aside, so that the eternal verities of religion: righteousness, truth, love, kindness, generosity, wisdom, etc., may be discussed as values in themselves, and as to how they may be applied in practice and assessed on their merits. Only in this way can the first steps towards a world ecumenicalism of all religions be undertaken – for a mere ecumenicalism of the Christian churches is a very limited exercise with a very limited purpose, bearing in mind the kind of global village in which we now all live.

The following chapters, therefore, are not concerned with a discussion of natural theology – and even less with revealed theology – but with the broader more urgent issue of religion in its widest context. It does have a purpose, however, which is very specific. It is a first step in calling religious leaders worldwide towards a universal system of ethics to which all might relate through the strength of their religious faith. If such a system of rational ethics clashes with the doctrines of any specific religion, then that may be a reason for stimulating theological discussion within that church. If such a system can be made to coexist with existing doctrines then all is well and good. In any case there is a need for a unifying religious body to help formulate and introduce such a universal system of ethics into religions worldwide.

Such an exercise and such a unifying world religious body cannot but help regenerate the spirituality of religion everywhere, since as I have argued, ethics must be the bond of any true religion in giving it purpose and meaning. At the same time, such an exercise would restore to religious leaders everywhere a new credibility in the eyes of their communities within the practical or political context.

6 – Religion must evolve with society

The lesson to be drawn from the contemporary situation of religion is that the latter must suit the age in which it exists. Religion needs to adapt to the society in which it finds itself in the same as philosophy, the arts, or technology. We live in an evolving world, and if religion fails to meet the *Zeitgeist* of the age, it may continue to retain a grudging respect, but at the same time it will lose its power as it is perceived as increasingly meaningless. If religion is to be credible and truthful, its first purpose must be to win the allegiance of the educated minority, i.e. of scientists and those in all branches of academia. And the problem today is that agnosticism, if not militant atheism, is most prevalent amongst the educated classes, who with good reason will not be budged from their rationalism and commonsense attitude to life.

The churches are aware of this situation, and over the years have produced a plethora of books on the nature of God in attempting to win over the hearts of intelligent sceptics, but all their efforts have failed as soon as they touch on the Christian message and its theological implications. The most famous of these books is perhaps John Robinson's *Honest To God*.[4] As a former Bishop of Woolwich, and subsequently, Dean of Trinity College, Cambridge, in his appeal to a wider audience, he probably extended the margins of liberalism to their fullest extent within the restraining limits of Christian doctrine. Whilst

---

[4] Published by SCM Press in 1963 and frequently reprinted.

the book generated considerable controversy, and was repudiated as heretical by fundamentalists and Evangelicals alike, it fails in its purpose in convincing the honest seeker after truth. Robinson based the leading theories of his book on the theology of Paul Tillich (1886-1965) and Dietrich Bonhoeffer (1906-1945), but despite the authority and the integrity of the ethical purpose of these thinkers, the intellectual gymnastics which needed to be employed are not sufficient in demonstrating the existence of the deity.

The outcome is that religion in the West – at least in Europe – is either pushed from the minds of the majority as an irrelevance, or is regarded in a hypocritical light, i.e. the tenets of the faith are accepted with an unthinking attitude, and this amounts to a nonchalance which takes the seriousness out of the significance of faith. If any religion is to be serious, i.e. regarded as a life-giving influence above all other values, it must be faith-based. And here we must describe exactly what we mean by the nature of faith.

7 – The deist interpretation of faith

Faith is not only a wonderful quality, it is a prerequisite for everyday existence. It brings out at all times a sense of certainty, security, and peace of mind, in so many spheres of life. It is always reassuring to know that two and two make four, and that we can anticipate the cause and effect of all the actions we take on a daily basis. But faith is not something which exists *in itself* as an independent quality – or at least, it should not. It develops through experience and factual knowledge, and just as faith is essential in the world of practicality, so also is its opposite, the quality of Mistrust. If we could not mistrust the reliability of the ageing electrical appliance; or the fairness of the weather; or the charms of the snake-oil salesman, our lives would soon be thrown into every kind of difficulty.

When faith is applied to the realm of religion, however, it seems to take up quite a different meaning, although the word remains the same and has not changed its semantic definition.

The real or core meaning of the word still stands as "complete trust or confidence," although in deference to theological gymnastics, a number of subsidiary interpretations are allowed a mention. For example, a "spiritual apprehension of divine truth apart from proof,"[5] is entered as an acceptable definition. What this really means is summed up in the curious phrase, "the suspension of belief," and this flies in the face of the proper understanding of faith as something based on experience or factual knowledge. It is in fact a blatant call to credulity and irrationality.

When, therefore, the religiously inclined begin to fret over their "lack of faith" in accepting the virgin birth, or the doctrine of the Trinity, or even over the existence of God, they begin to reproach themselves for an apparent unidentifiable "weakness" of character, or an inexplicable lack of will, or some other mysterious aptitude, which is not denied others amongst their religious friends. Such people should have no reasons for self-reproach, for their better or healthier selves are trying to tell them that there is a *reason* for their "lack of faith."

This lack of faith is symptomatic of nothing less than that their sense of reason is trying to break through a wall of prejudice and superstition, instilled through nurture during their years of upbringing. The defensive voice of mistrust is struggling to attract their better judgement. This is the crisis point with which many millions are confronted at some time in their lives. Are they to surrender with a thoughtless irrationality to some system of organised religion, and live a lie as its slaves forever more; or are they to listen to their rational selves in maintaining an independence of mind?

The majority in today's world choose the latter course. But most do not reach this decision through a spiritual crisis of any kind. Such crises remain the privilege of the minority comprising the very religiously inclined. The majority adopt a more matter-of-fact attitude to the question of religion. In their apathy they hardly give the issue a passing thought. But on the other hand, they have no wish or intention to betray disrespect

---

[5] *The Oxford Encyclopedic Dictionary*, op. cit., p. 508.

to the Church or sect of their forebears. Providing they are free to keep a distance from religion, they are prepared to offer it a distant acknowledgement and even claim a nominal membership of the belief into which they were supposedly born.

8 – Religion and the rationalists' disappointment

Whilst the unthinking majority choose to keep religion at a distance from their lives, for the most part as an irrelevance, there exists a fair proportion of the socially concerned and thinking population, who would willingly embrace the precepts of religion if only it met with the sensibility of their reason. It is probable that there are many millions in the world today who would fully commit themselves to God and religion if only faith would match up with reason.

If I recount two examples of personal experience, in hoping to encounter a religious movement of integrity, they might also illustrate what millions of others have also experienced in a similar way, as well as reflecting a common attitude to the question of religion. As a young man in his late teens, somewhat over 50 years ago, I was attracted by posters and display advertisements in the press, calling for a campaign for *Moral Rearmament*. There was nothing in the advertising which indicated the organisation behind such a campaign, other than that it was well-funded by powerful financial backers, but as it seemed to promise a good cause, my curiosity and hopes were aroused, and so I decided to attend a rally in a large hall in London's Regent Street.

The rally began fortuitously enough in hopeful anticipation, amongst a crowd of well-meaning people, and the speakers moved the hearts of their audience with stirring rhetoric. But after an hour or so, all was suddenly revealed, and from a spirit of elation I was moved to a feeling of disgust and disappointed hope. I awoke to feel I had been called to the meeting on false pretences, in listening to a tissue of lies and superstition. The campaign was nothing more than an attempt to propagate the Christian message, and I was left with a feeling of contempt for the trickery of the Evangelists who had planned the meeting. Not only had my time and bus money been wastefully used, and not only had dishonest means been used to get me into the hall in the first place, but my intelligence as a rational and (hopefully) enlightened human being had been grossly insulted.

The second experience occurred within the last ten years. As a committee member of an association holding a series of monthly lectures, I was asked to meet an appointed speaker and bring him to the meeting place. The said person was a prominent Cambridge physicist, who had been invited to talk on the nature of God, but beyond those facts, at the time, I knew nothing more about his background. I felt optimistic in anticipating a talk supported with learned argument and guided by practical commonsense. What else would one expect from a distinguished physicist?

On meeting him there was nothing to indicate he should be regarded in any other light than the highest respect. He was a bespectacled, bald-headed, ageing man, somewhat over-corpulent – but I excused this on the Claret at the top table of his College – and in every way he revealed the respectability of the Oxbridge academic. He fumbled over his coins for the parking meter, but I quickly relieved him of this embarrassment by paying the fee, and when we got into conversation on the way to the hall, there was nothing to betray anything wanting in his soundness of mind. During the lecture which followed, however, I was soon disabused of my expectations in listening to new and interesting ideas on the nature of the deity, for I was quick to discover he was peddling all the old myths and superstitions.

9 – The clandestine financing of religion

After this experience, I was not merely filled with disgust, but felt that I had been confronted by *positive evil*. How could an educated man (or woman), deeply embedded in the scientific spirit, be relied upon to have any integrity for the truth when he declares his belief in the Trinity, the Virgin birth, the

Resurrection, and the other age old doctrines which cannot possibly be supported by honest reasoning? Has he thrown away all honest argument for reasoning to the wind? Has he no responsibility to the cause of learning and progress? Has he no moral sense in standing by the knowledge, he acquired as a physicist and repudiating that which goes beyond physics – i.e. *metaphysics*? It has to be said that more is expected of a physicist in defending the demonstrable truth, than would be expected of, say, a philosopher or other thinker not experienced in the world of science. For these reasons, I could only see evil springing from the religious teaching of such a man. I could only let out a cry of pain, and in paraphrasing the words of Hamlet, exclaim, "Get thee to a laboratory!"

Since that event, I have learned something more about the man in question. His name is the Reverend Sir John Polkinghorne, a member of a small group of British scientists, who have become notorious as propagandists of the Christian message. Richard Dawkins has written about that minority of great scientists who are religious in the honest or Einsteinian sense, but when he turns to those scientists who are religious in the "full traditional sense," he scathingly records that, "Among contemporary British scientists, the same three names crop up with the likeable familiarity of senior partners in a firm of Dickensian lawyers: Peacocke, Stannard and Polkinghorne. All three have either won the Templeton Prize or are on the Templeton Board of Trustees. After amicable discussions with all of them, both in public and private, I remain baffled, not so much by their belief in a cosmic lawgiver of some kind, as by their belief in the details of the Christian religion: resurrection, forgiveness of sins and all."[6]

Perhaps it should be explained that the Templeton Foundation is a body, which in the words of Richard Dawkins awards, "a very large sum of money given annually ... usually to a scientist who is prepared to say something nice about religion."[7] Elsewhere, in writing about the skulduggery of the

---

[6] Richard Dawkins, *The God Delusion*, Bantam Press, 2006, p. 99.
[7] Ibid., p. 19.

body in financing the Christian message through the names of prominent personalities, he refers to the "infamous Templeton Foundation."[8]

10 – The mendacious environment of churchgoing

Before turning to the topic of deism as the religion without falsehood, perhaps I should further clarify my personal feelings as to why I saw the Christian individuals and organisations described in the two episodes above as sources of such evil. I have always felt, as indeed, I believe many millions of others must feel alike, that herding large groups of people into an enclosed space, on a regular basis, for the purpose of performing a series of repetitious activities, is demeaning to humanity and insulting to his intelligence.

The repetition of the same prayers, and the singing of the same psalms and the too-familiar hymns, and the herd-like rituals of supposedly like-minded people, and the tiresome exercise of alternate standing, sitting, and genuflecting for extended periods, until the thighs ache and the knees are unbearably sore, becomes meaningless because of its enforcement as unthinking habit. One may enjoy the singing of familiar tunes, or listening to the beauty of a chant, or that of a sonorous delivery in reading a lesson or prayer, but whoever bothers to really comprehend the *meaning* of the spoken words – if they are consciously heard in the first place?

The underlying motive behind such ritual and such repetition is only to enforce dogma, and was only designed by the church in instilling the discipline of outward form on our heathen ancestors, so they might *nominally* be accepted as believers into the new faith. Such ritual has no more purpose than that: i.e. the enforcement of church authority on an ignorant mass, not that the mind may be controlled (for nothing can ensure that) but that outward behaviour may be monitored to the satisfaction of the priesthood.

---

[8] Ibid., p. 344.

Churchgoing is therefore not an educational activity, apart from the sermon which nowadays hardly occupies a fifth of the service, and consequently, the church service has little more value than as a bonding mechanism of those declaring their membership of a particular group. An indefinable feeling of religiosity may be strengthened in those truly committed to the faith, but that in itself does not make them better people, and it certainly does not raise their intelligence so they might usefully apply their intellect in leaving the world a better place than they found it.

The repetitious nature of the church service is demeaning to humankind, since it tends to numb the senses with rituals used to enhance myths, miracles and unbelievable stories, which can rarely be intelligibly interpreted in more than a metaphorical meaning. Meanwhile, the priests or pastors are privy to a huge body of theology which pertains to give credence to the impossible, but because of its complexity, it is seldom communicated to the lay congregation, and so the entire aspect of the churchgoing environment becomes equivocal and mendacious, and is definitely anti-rational, anti-intellectual, and anti-sceptical in the healthy honest meaning of that word. In the final resort, when all intellectual gymnastics have been exhausted – as they always are – the church is obliged to fall back on the need for *faith* in the bad sense of that word.

Hence the organised church treats their members as little better than cattle, to be driven this way and that, sometimes with threats or trickery, but always to take up their same places in the cowshed where they may be relied upon to perform their expected function. How, then, can the best men and women in the advanced industrialised economies of the 21st century be expected to waste their time and energies in such repetitious mind-demeaning activities? It is not so much amoral as immoral.

In a world of rapid change and increasing crises, it is intelligence and this-worldly action which is called-for and not the *faith* of other-worldly religion. The real evil of the organised churches is to be seen in that aspect of their teaching which entails a turning-away from the problems of our terrestrial existence. The ethics of deism is that its God commands that humankind must maximise and utilise his intelligence in saving this world as a moral imperative.

CHAPTER 2

RELIGION WITHOUT FALSEHOOD

*"**Deist**:* a man who follows no particular religion but only acknowledges the existence of God, without any other article of faith."

Dr. Johnson's *Dictionary*, 1755.

1 – "Faith" misused by the churches

In returning to the question of religious faith, it will be found that two leading themes of this book are, firstly, that the great organised world churches, as we find them today, are a discredit to both the concept and practice of serious religion; and secondly, that attempts to apply the principles of faith to these same churches, devalue and make ridiculous the idea of faith itself. It therefore follows that if a person is touched with doubt in regard to making a religious commitment, his wise and only choice is to avoid taking that fateful leap into the dark.

It is only due to the psychological pressures of the churches themselves, and their willingness to exploit feelings of guilt – often when there is no cause for guilt in the first place – that so many become trapped in a life of falsehood and wrong-thinking. Once that fatal commitment has been taken, the individual is expected to leave his intelligence and better judgement behind, in exchange for blind faith and obedience, and an authority which may take him eventually he knows not where.

It should be noted at this point, that leading deists until the present time, most notably Voltaire and Thomas Paine, have repudiated the idea of faith in favour of *reason*, but such a stand is naturally dependent on the definition which is given to the concept of faith. And that is the reason we have devoted so much space to the discussion of faith in clarifying its core meaning as complete trust and confidence, and nothing more. Our purpose has been to separate the idea of faith from the notion of *revelation*, where the word has been devalued and used, in what we consider, is a twisted sense.

There are also four other reasons for clarifying the true meaning of faith: firstly, in giving – and seeming to give – a greater certitude to the truths of deism; secondly, in further removing it from the idea of atheism; thirdly, in more closely associating deism as either truly religious or a religion in its own right; and fourthly, and most significantly, as a spiritual springboard in attracting and maintaining the heightened commitment of millions of thinking and well-meaning people throughout the world to the cause of deism. All this is necessary as a preparation in elaborating on the nature of deism as described below.

This is not to suggest that an organised deism should seek to stir up mass emotionalism through exploiting crowd psychology in evangelistic-style rallies. Such tactics, seeking to exploit the irrational brain cells, would be contrary to both the spirit and ethics of deism. It would fill them with aversion and disgust, for it would remind them that the same psychology was used at the Nuremberg rallies, and the fact that the two causes are different is irrelevant when the methods in themselves are wrong. An organised deism may indeed call meetings in halls, theatres, or stadia, but they would need to be held with a quiet dignity, and they would need to be addressed by speakers with human qualities in conveying balance, humour, a subtlety of mind, and an appeal to reason.

2 – Evils stemming from Revelation in today's world

For the thinking person seeking to lead a moral and religious life, it is therefore quite unnecessary to sacrifice the intellectual freedom necessary in commitment to the blind faith of a revealed religion. There is an alternative path for enlightened men and women, and this of course, entails a commitment to the cause of deism. Deism is best and most succinctly defined as "One who believes in the existence of a

God or Supreme Being but denies revealed religion, basing his belief on the light of nature and reason."[9]

Deism has been called into existence for two reasons: firstly, because its claims are based on the rational truth, and hence do not attempt to impose the jiggery-pokery of unsupportable arguments in upholding impossible myths or stories; and secondly, because the deceit arising from religions of revelation have led directly to so many unmitigated evils in world history. It may be contended in response to the latter, that we are only referring to historical situations and not the present, but this is untrue. The suspension of belief in the sphere of religious life in our own time, has led to the rise and extinction of sects which have witnessed the massacre of hundreds of innocent committed members by their own leaders. Witness the bloody record of Jim Jones (of the People's Temple) or David Koresh and the Waco incident.

Then, again, in the sphere of political power – on which we are all dependent irrespective of choice – it is a dire situation when our leaders claim to be led by the Word of God. It is frightening, since the purely irrational takes over in replacing commonsense – and moreover, takes over in the name of a Supreme and irrefutable authority. If it was not for the belief in revelation, all the suffering, the economic collapse, and the deaths of thousands, might have been avoided in Iraq. But it was the perverted religiosity of two men in two countries, each working within a small caucus of individuals, which led directly to all the evils of the Iraq War.

3 – Some accepted definitions of deism

Deism makes no unreasonable claims. The deist, and most renowned scientist of the 20th century, Albert Einstein, declared that, "My religion consists of a humble admiration of the illimitable superior spirit who reveals himself in the slight details we are able to perceive with our frail and feeble minds. That deeply emotional conviction of the presence of a superior

---

[9]   *Webster's Encyclopedic Dictionary*, 1941.

reasoning power, which is revealed in the incomprehensible universe, forms my idea of God. ... I cannot imagine a God who rewards and punishes the objects of his creation, whose purposes are modelled after our own – a God, in short, who is but a reflection of human frailty. It is enough for me to contemplate the mystery of conscious life perpetuating itself through all eternity, to reflect upon the marvellous structure of the universe which we can dimly perceive and to try humbly to comprehend even an infinitesimal part of the intelligence manifested in nature.[10] ... To sense that behind anything that can be experienced there is a something that our mind cannot grasp and whose beauty and sublimity reaches us only indirectly and as a feeble reflection, this is religiousness. In this sense I am religious."[11]

Three other recent statements on deism, all taken from authoritative sources, may be quoted in further clarifying the meaning of the term: "We believe that God designed and created the world, and governs it through natural laws that can be discovered through reasoning, observation, and experience. We feel that God does not reveal himself to us through inspired or revealed texts or by supernatural means, but through creation itself."[12] – "I freely believe in God as being discovered through nature and reason, rejecting revealed religion and its authority over humanity. I believe all humans are equal. Further, as God has not shown favour for one people over another and has given us all that we need, that we should follow God's example and give to others as we can."[13] – "Members of the United Deist Community hold the belief that God is discovered through Reason ... but the task of discovery is never over. We each pursue a lifelong intellectual odyssey; harvesting from the tree of knowledge all the wisdom that we can. Members are encouraged to participate in fellowship with other members, continuing the search for Truth together. Our open minds and

---

[10] Taken from www.religioustolerance.org/deism.htm.
[11] Quoted from Richard Dawkins, op. cit., p. 19.
[12] Taken from the Peace Dale Christian Deist Fellowship's website.
[13] Taken from the United Deist Church's website.

open hearts are changing the world with love and deeds, as no other religion can."[14]

4 – The character of deism

Deism is not organised as a church, and because it teaches self-reliance and to question authority, irrespective of the cost, through its intrinsic characteristics, it has little inclination to move towards the status of a highly organised body. Its adherents meet in groups on an informal basis, for discussion and the mutual confirmation of their beliefs, but they have no theology, or appointed priests or elders, and so no hierarchy in imposing any kind of authority. Consequently, there is a wide differentiation of personal beliefs amongst its members. Those organised religious bodies most closely reflecting the spirit of deism are the Unitarians and the Society of Friends (Quakers), down-to-earth, practical people, successful in business, with a strong intellectual streak, and seldom averse to freethinking or the progress of science.

Until the present time, the nearest text which summarises the religious philosophy of deism remains Thomas Paine's the *Age of Reason*, Part I of which was published in 1794, just before his arrest by Robespierre, and Part II was written whilst a prisoner in Paris in 1795, and subsequently published in 1796. Another important work is Immanuel Kant's, *Religion Within The Limits of Reason Alone*, published in 1792-94, which was severely disapproved of by the Prussian king, Frederick William II; banned by the Lutheran church towards the end of the 18th century; placed on the Vatican's Index in 1827; banned by the Soviets in 1928; and, all copies held in Spanish libraries, ordered to be burnt in 1939 by the Caudillo, Generalissimo Franco. Amongst the religions of the world, it is surprising that deists still comprise a tiny minority of individuals amongst a world still dominated by the arrogance of theological intolerance and stupidity. In Chapter 4 we shall explain the reasons for this.

---

[14] Taken from the United Deist Community website.

Because deists form such a minority, and because their voice is rarely heard in religious or intellectual circles, and because they are unorganised as a body, it is not surprising that deism is often misunderstood and grossly misinterpreted, even by those in academia. Before elaborating on the philosophical foundations of deism, as a basis for its regeneration in the 21st century, I therefore want to correct several false perceptions concerning its reality.

5 – Common misinterpretations of deism

The first is the common assumption that deism equals atheism. In the words of J.M. Robertson, it is true that "Before 'deism' came into English vogue, the names for unbelief, even deistic, were simply 'infidelity' and 'atheism' – e.g. Bishop Fotherby's *Atheamastix* (1622), Baxter's *Unreasonableness of Infidelity* (1655), and, *Reasons of the Christian Religion* (1667) passim. Bishop Stillingfleet's *Letter to a Deist* (1677) appears to be the first published attack on deism by name. His *Origenes Sacrae* (1662) deals chiefly with deistic views, but calls unbelievers in general 'atheists.'"[15]

By the first half of the 18th century, however, by which time English deism had become fully fledged as an intellectual movement, the term "atheism" was not used as a basis for rational critique, but was only flung at deism as a term of abuse. It was used on the grounds that anything breaking the bounds of heterodoxy, not only deserved the epithet of atheism, but was atheism in actuality.

This brings to mind the words of that ridiculous, narrow-minded and ever-moralising cleric, the Reverend Thwackum, who on one occasion was discovered by Tom Jones cowering stark naked in a cupboard in a trollop's bedroom, when he exclaimed, "When I mention religion, I mean the Christian religion; and not only the Christian religion, but the Protestant religion; and not only the Protestant religion but the Church of

---

[15]   J.M. Robertson, *A Short History of Freethought Ancient & Modern*, Watts & Co., 2nd ed., 1906, Vol. I, p. 4.

England."[16] Fielding ironically remarks that, "Thwackum was for doing justice, and leaving mercy to heaven."[17] Such a man in his myopia and arrogance would doubtless have identified deism as "atheism."

Richard Dawkins in his book, *The God Delusion*, presents a distorted view of deism which calls for refutation. He either misapprehends the nature of deism, or if he refrains from disparaging it, he is certainly intent on putting it in the shade in clearing the way for out-and-out atheism. Firstly, he describes deism as a "watered-down theism."[18] This is a false perception. Both terms refer to a belief in God, although theism is usually understood as a "supernatural belief." But if we conclude that deism is a more accurate or true interpretation of the meaning of God, then clearly it conveys a wrong impression if described as a "watered-down theism." Hence such a description is an unwarranted slur on the significance and superior value of deism when put against its comparison.

Secondly, he asserts that deists believe in a "supernatural intelligence,"[19] an adjective with which I would strongly disagree. Deists do not, or should not, give credence to the "magical" or "mystical," or to forces "above the laws of nature," all definitions of which fall under the category of the *supernatural*.[20]

Thirdly, he describes the deist God as "one whose activities were confined to setting up the laws that govern the universe in the first place. The deist God never intervenes thereafter, and certainly has no specific intent in human affairs."[21] Somewhat later on in the book, he continues ironically, "The deist God is a physicist to end all physics, the alpha and omega of mathematicians, the apotheosis of designers; a hyper-engineer who set up the laws and constants of the universe, fine-tuned them with exquisite precision and

---

[16] Henry Fielding, *Tom Jones*, Bk. 3, Ch. 3.
[17] Ibid., Bk, 3m Ch. 10.
[18] Richard Dawkins, op. cit., p. 18.
[19] Ibid, p. 18.
[20] *Oxford Encyclopedic Dictionary*, op. cit., p. 1453.
[21] Richard Dawkins, op. cit., p. 18.

foreknowledge, detonated what we would now call the hot big bang, retired and was never heard of again."[22]

All this, of course, is an absurdity, but in fairness to Dawkins, it has to be admitted that deism is often carelessly described in dictionaries and brief entries in guides to philosophy, as belief in a deity who establishes the universe before sinking into a kind of retirement and so leaving the universe to its own devices. This is a parody of deism on a par with the joke of a music-hall comedian. Why should a deity bother to establish a universe and then turn his back on his own creation? Is there not a whiff of callousness and irresponsibility in such an attitude? And anyway, why should a God choose to relinquish the power which is already in his grasp? The confusion arises over the concept of God.

6 – A definitive interpretation of deism

The deist God is not a mere person, with the human attributes of anger, jealousy, and revenge, like the God of the three Abrahamic religions. He does not sit on a throne, crowned, with golden vestments, and a long white beard, scowling before the flattery of a host of adoring nubile angels, singing hymns for all eternity. The deist God is infinitely superior to such a simplistic concept. The deist God is an Essence or Entity, and if described as a Being, this is meant as Existence rather than as a consciously responding mind with feelings, as can only emerge from a material life. And this Being, Essence, or abstract Entity is purely ethical in its nature.

The deistic concept of God advanced in this book is simple but irrefutable in its reality as truth. It makes no attempt to stretch the imagination of the mundane mind, or the credulity of the sceptical, since it is based on self-evident factors as well as on the demonstrative proofs of science. God needs to be comprehended as the coming into being of the good. His existence is not only demonstrated through evolution or natural selection, but through the progress of society towards a better

---

[22] Ibid., p. 38.

and more ethical life. Of course there are periods when there is retrogression in society, just as there is in natural selection, but these are aberrations or abnormalities which temporarily – even if sometimes for extended periods – interrupt the progress of the universe.

Humankind is not necessarily the highest form of life in the universe – and certainly does not comprise its centre – although for the time being he may know no higher form of life's existence. And neither should humankind be regarded as a specially favoured species, deserving exclusive favours. This is because is he part of a greater interconnected ecosystem, all of which comprises the existence of God, and all of which deserves respect within an egalitarianism of materialistic terrestrial phenomena. This, of course, is a reminder that humankind may doom himself to self-destruction, if he so wills it in defying the nature and goodness of God.

Hence evolution or progress within the universe presents a "snakes and ladders" scenario, and this in part explains what we mean by the egalitarianism of materialistic phenomena. And progress, it should be noted, is not a lineal or logical process, but proceeds through stimulus and response, or the Hegelian trinity of thesis, antithesis and synthesis. It is a process entailing struggle, pain, and even destruction, and so is the growth of the human being, if we substitute the loss of childish illusions in the place of destruction.

The essence of God, and the ever-present potential of the coming-into-being of the good, is present in all things and omnipotent throughout the universe, but it needs to be understood that the Supreme Being works within the natural laws of existence, and therefore cannot be invoked or summoned at our will, with the pull of a bell-rope, like an ordinary butler. It is a God which expects – demands even – our absolute obedience, but not to a list of man-made commandments deceitfully attributed to a deity, but to our evolving and God-given intelligence.

We are indeed dependent on God, as manifested throughout the universe, but it is a dependence relying on our creativity, knowledge, skill, and moreover anything else, on our ethical sense or good judgement in all life's decision-making. In following God's Word (if we take this term to mean his authority) it is the duty of every individual to develop his or her full potential in the spheres of physical, intellectual, spiritual, and ethical life; and in conjunction with this, to integrate with the good of one's community and with humanity at large, in the struggle for a better world.

7 – Towards the ethical life and a peaceful death

A brief note should be made in distinguishing the spiritual from the ethical life: for the first refers to the will and intuitive sense and general disposition of a person; whilst the second refers to the critical and objective faculties of the mind in deciding what constitutes right and wrong. The God-observing individual (for the term is psychologically more appropriate than "God-fearing") will ensure that his spiritual life conforms to his more rational ethical sense. In other words, in a changing and complex world, where we may have been exposed to questionable values in early life, it is important that the heart should be subordinated or corrected by the mind.

The ethical life demands an active as contrasted with a passive existence, for only the first can test our attributes through experience, and only then can we practice and improve on our wanting characteristics. And such a life entails a social existence, for human beings are social animals. A passive or contemplative existence, on the contrary, may be excusable – indeed, in certain circumstances, may be admirable for certain individuals – but only when they are past middle age, and wish to instil the experiences of a lifetime in a work of wisdom for posterity.

A passive or contemplative life for the young is merely a retreat from life – a running away from reality, and hence is an immoral (and unhealthy) course to follow. All these observations stem directly from the deistic nature of God as firmly committed to the ethical values of a scientific or this-worldly existence. The first duty of the healthy-minded and successful being is concern for the present world. Heaven should be subordinated to a secondary place in our consciousness –for that is how God would want it. Naturally, when approaching death, or when ill or in old age, it may be apt to reflect on a past life and the possible prospects for our future memory in the minds of others or in that of a timeless cosmic existence. That is excusable.

But an obsessive concern with the possibility of an afterlife is morbid, and often reflects an inner dissatisfaction with our present earthly life. Hence it casts aspersions on the life which God has granted us, and for this reason should be resisted in exploring the disturbance of our own psyche. We should then seek to improve our lives by removing the unhappiness at its core. In thinking about or approaching the reality of death, we should therefore think backwards rather than forwards: i.e. to the concern of completing those things we have left undone; to mending broken friendships or relationships; and to seeking our peace with the world as we find it.

If we achieve these things, we will die with contented hearts. To merely look forward, in fretting about the possibilities of the future, is a futile cause of anxiety. In facing the prospect of extinction it is preferable to be consoled by Lucretius, than by the insolent threats of the Apostles with their prospects of damnation. Although Lucretius accepted the gods, he sought to rid us of our superstitious and religious fears of death. See especially Book III of his philosophical poem *On the Nature of Things* (*De rerum natura*) which anticipates the deism of a later era.

Because deism conforms to the reality of human nature, it looks askance at the individual who attempts to separate himself from the rest of humanity, or who claims to be seen in a different light from others. How insufferable, selfish, and psychologically disturbed are those Biblical prophets claiming superiority over the rest of their race, and claiming a special dispensation from God!

As man is a social animal, deism lays greater emphasis on social ethics than on the ethics of the individual soul. Both are important, but only social ethics, through political and democratic mechanisms can hope to improve the total lot of humanity. An ethics which contributes to the happiness of all contributes also to the happiness of the One. If the One, the lonely tortured soul, would seek the happiness of all, in his generosity and greater breadth of interest, he would also find a greater happiness for himself.

Because humankind is essentially a social animal, social life is essential to both psychic and physical or bodily health, and contrariwise, isolation or loneliness contributes to illness or disease. Dr. Robert Wilson of Rush University Medical Center, Chicago, after a 6-year research project, has demonstrated in an article published in the February 2007 issues of the journal, *Archives of General Psychiatry*, that persistently lonely people are twice as likely to develop Alzheimers or dementia, and are otherwise vulnerable to the deleterious effects of age-related neuropathological disease than their more sociable peers. It therefore follows that deism should not only place a greater emphasis on the moral imperative of sociability, but should also place a greater emphasis on social ethics, as on balance warranting a priority over personal ethics as a matter for consideration.

8 – Our first duty is salvation in the present world, not the next

All churches have their own distinctive outlook on the terrestrial world, and these differ somewhat one from the other, but most are too fatalistic, tending to promote the attitude, "Give thanks for your blessings, keep your head down, and accept the world as it is." Deists, on the contrary, insist on the need to *change* the world, for that is the command of an ethically-based Supreme Being who is immanent in the world, and all its activity, and the decision-making of humanity.

Our first duty should be to ensure salvation in the present world and not the next. God should not be regarded as a distant sky-dwelling Being, in a universe divided into separate spheres of influence, where power needs to be negotiated between Heaven, Earth, and Hell. This is the simplistic view of many simple ordinary people, even though it may vary from accepted theological ideas.

Despite the minimalism of its theology, it should be noted that deism is as spiritually enriching as any organised or established religion, and since it is the only religion which may be accepted as based on truth by many millions of educated and sceptical people in the modern industrialised world, it remains their only possibility for experiencing the spiritual benefits of religion. The motivating power of deism is to be found in its rationally-based ethics, and once this is accepted, the idea of God as essence manifested throughout the universe can begin to exert its spiritual power. This is discovered through the mystery arising through the awe at our own limitations, and the infinity of knowledge which we cannot hope to comprehend in a lifetime. This allows for our speculation on the nature of God, through the process of metaphysics, and this in turn broadens our spiritual enlightenment.

This definitive interpretation of the Supreme Being evokes a refreshing, healthy, truthful and optimistic view of God's nature. It is stripped of the mythic fog and false intellectual gymnastics which form an impenetrable barrier between the upright individual and the clarity of his understanding of God. It rids religion of all that is inessential, pretentious, pompous, and all that is distractingly (even intentionally) complex in its theological arguments. Deism evokes a religion which is frank and open in its integrity. The proselytisers of the great organised religious faiths need to be very circumspect with regard to the individuals they approach, and they need to assess a personality in advance of presenting the message, and if they are not entirely without sensitivity, they are usually apprehensive of the response they may expect.

Deists need have none of these hang-ups, irrespective of whomsoever they approach. Their message has such clarity of meaning, and is in such perfect conformance with science and reason, that they may approach the physicist, the lawyer, the engineer, the hospital consultant – and even the learned divine, all on an equal footing. The deist need never risk compromising his intelligence or zeal in propagating his beliefs, and even when confronting the confirmed atheist, he may nonetheless enjoy a mutually stimulating and constructive discussion in a friendly environment over a bottle of Claret.

The imperative and social significance of deism is that it commands in the name of the deity that humankind should maximise his intelligence in resolving all his earthly problems. Although it does not exclude entirely the possibility of resorting to prayer (see the final chapter of this book) it looks askance on those who would use religion as a convenient petitionary mechanism for their wants, or as a message board for God. Our heads were given to us by God, so that we might use them, and not that we might wait and expect another to act on our behalf. God is not our servant but we are *His*.

In ages past, religious celibates and recluses across the globe, always had the reputation of being amongst the laziest people in society. I well remember, many years ago, when a slot machine for booklets in a Roman church, close to the Forum, failed to deliver the purchase I had made, and when I approached a monk lazily sunning himself on the steps outside, he merely threw up his arms in irritated exasperation. Just at that moment, a young man and his wife were passing by, and on witnessing the incident, to my sudden astonishment, he railed at the monk as a dirty idle ne'er-do-well, who had nothing better to do than rest his arse, and that he had better return me my money.

Taken aback, but still remaining seated, the monk drew out a handful of money from his cloak, and grudgingly replaced the coin I had lost. It was the first of several occasions when I witnessed the contempt with which many Romans regarded the clergy. The value of deism is that it strives to distance itself from all forms of corruption, or situations which might tend to corrupt the character or modes of right thinking. Humankind cannot hope to be honest to God, until he is first honest to himself, and that means refraining from accepting any so-called ultimate truths until his intellect can accept them with crystal clarity.

CHAPTER 3

THE PRACTICAL WORK OF DEISM

"Religion should extinguish strife,
And make a calm of human life;
But friends that chance to differ
On points which God has left at large,
How fiercely they will meet and charge,
No combatants are stiffer!"

William Cowper, *Friendship*, 1, 133.

1 – An over-arching religion

It is important to consider deism as an organising body of activity. Although deism is a belief system, it is not in any sense a church, and it is probable that the independent spirit of deism, together with the sweet calmness of its rationality, would resist the idea of formation into a formalised or bureaucratic body. The most that can be hope for – and it may be more than sufficient – is the organisation of voluntary bodies, meeting for discussion, lectures, and on a social basis, in confirming their commitment to the only true God with meaning to enlightened people in the third millennium.

Deism may be best perceived and propagated as an over-arching religion, which through belief in the existence of the Supreme Being, is the minimum requirement for a religious body of teaching. Deism is that which sets a clear separation between religion and non-religion, or believers and non-believers. As such, in the modern sceptical world in which we live today, where atheism predominates amongst the most intelligent classes of academia, deists and the teachings of deism, should be welcomed on a friendly basis by the enlightened leaders and adherents of all religions for the purpose of dialogue. The age is long past when sensible men and women of a religious persuasion can simply afford to dismiss the presence of deism, or simply attach to it the abusive epithet of "atheism."

2 – Proselytising amongst the "committed and "born again"

Deism may work on two levels: firstly, as an independent movement amongst its fully committed adherents, in forming groups, holding meetings, and publishing papers and books. Secondly, it may operate as a proselytising body amongst all other churches and sects. In this role it would need to work with sensitivity and understanding. As deists are rational and intelligent people, they must first achieve a comprehensive understanding of the theology of the church or sect they tend to approach, before attempting to convey their message.

Furthermore, it is necessary to attend the services of the actual church of those they intend to proselytise for several weeks at least, so they are afforded the opportunity to assess the temperament and opinions of the congregation in preparing a careful strategy. Deists should never be confrontational or dogmatic, for that is contrary to the open and liberal spirit of deism, and besides, it is counter-productive in the art of effective persuasion. Religion is always a matter of *feeling*, and feelings must be respected, and so the deist should always seek to project himself as warm-hearted but calm, socially relaxed but serious, with a gentle humour but full of consideration for those around him.

Through his easy and pleasant personality he should attract the friendship of others. Since his reasoning powers may be strong, he should resist the temptation of being inveigled too soon into a lively or deep discussion on religious matters, for he may then fall into a trap which has been set for him. In that event his cover may be blown, and leading members of the congregation may warn their brethren and sisters that a deist is in their midst who should be avoided for the salvation of their souls.

The early proselytising of a congregation or group should be done undercover, and the first expressions of the deist should be concerned with living a truthful life, and that beliefs, whatsoever they are, should be based in truth. Then the deist should express disdain for all superstition and its corruption of religion. Next, the deist should underline the importance of ethics, and that as a body of knowledge, it is an essential study for all those of a religious persuasion.

Few are likely to be contentious over the expression of any of the above sentiments made in an informal social environment over a cup of tea following a church service. But they may indeed lend to interesting and enlightening discussion, and unbeknown to themselves, Christian, Jewish, Islamic, or those of any other faith, may have taken the first steps towards a deistic view of existence. After some months, an observant congregation member may jokingly retort, "I do believe you are a deist," to which the latter may good-humouredly reply, "Yes, I confess I am at heart, but at the same time I love and respect your church."

In answer to the question, "Do you accept the teachings of Christ/Mohammed/Buddha, etc.,?" the prudent answer should be, "I accept the ethically-based aspects of his teaching, but not the myths or supernatural theology built around his personality." Such a circumspect response allows for the qualification that not all the teachings of the said leader might have been ethical from an objective viewpoint, and indeed, no religious leader has been morally infallible in every respect – not even Jesus Christ.[23] The deist must never surrender to the weakness of giving a dishonest answer, but on the other hand, he must always strive to respect the sensibility of others.

Eventually the deist will have so entrenched himself as an accepted member of the congregation, and have so won over the friendship and confidence of its members, that no one would wish or even think of turning him away. He may thenceforward be perceived in a somewhat ambiguous light, i.e. as "not entirely of their faith," and one who in his turn may be a good prospect for conversion, but he will seldom be regarded with ill-will. In other situations, the deist will simply sense when it is timely to openly admit his deism, whilst nonetheless retaining the authority to continue his religious mission.

---

[23] In this respect, see especially pages 9-14 of Bertrand Russell's book, *Why I am Not A Christian*, Allen & Unwin, 1957.

3 – Proselytising amongst the lukewarm

The above situations illustrate the more difficult tasks of the deist when proselytising amongst the free churches, with their evangelising "born again" traditions, or perhaps when approaching Roman Catholics, Islamists, or Ultra-Orthodox Jews. As soon as the deist approaches the Anglican churches, an easier task confronts him. This is due to the fact that perhaps 80% of Anglican communicants are already unknowingly of a deistic disposition. The Church of England is certainly amongst the broadest, most humane, liberal, and relaxed of all the Christian denominations.

For most, it is little more than a social bonding association of friendly souls with the slimmest knowledge or interest in theological matters. Whilst church services may leave an indefinable sense of well-being, its sermons offer an excuse for a gentle snooze, and most are impatient for tea and biscuits in the vestry afterwards to exchange town or village gossip. In such an environment, with its declining memberships, any additions to the congregation are always welcome, and the deist will soon attach himself to the more committed Christians amongst their number, and the fact of his religiosity (whatever that might be) is hardly likely to offend the latitudinarian attitudes of those he encounters.

The openly deistic communicant will win and maintain the friendship and respect of Anglicans on the grounds of his serious religiosity and search for truth, and also because of his declared belief in a Supreme Being. Nonetheless, the Church of England is in crisis, and its clergy are far from complacent. The main issues of conflict are too well known, and anyway, are irrelevant to the subject matter of this book, but the crisis of belief, which receives little publicity, is of far more significance to the future of the church. If it was not for the breadth and generosity of the Church, in allowing for such a diversity of views, it might already have splintered and contracted to a fraction of its present size within the last decade or two.

The well-meaning, realistic, and usually reasonable clergy of the Church of England, are therefore amongst the best and prime prospects for the cause of deism, and once they are committed deists, they are likely to prove its finest and most effective propagandists. However, this is not to suggest that deists should seek to wean away the Anglican clergy from their Church. Quite the contrary strategy should be used. A practical approach and respect for economics should be maintained. Nothing is more pitiful or useless than an unemployed priest, and this is realised by the clergy themselves. The cause of deism may be far better propagated through the clergy retaining their livings, and preaching the message of deism from their accustomed pulpits.

They need not, of course, openly declare themselves as deists. They need advance no further in their covert teaching of deist views than many of their Anglican forebears in the 18th century. In taking the example of one such divine, it has been recorded that in the five published volumes of sermons of the eminent Scottish minister, Dr. Hugh Blair (1718-1800), the name of Jesus Christ gains not a single mention. And Blair was not alone amongst the learned divines of his age, in this respect.

And like their 18th century forebears, today's clergy may continue the ritual and practices of the Church in the understanding that these have nothing more than an agreeable allegorical meaning. But even as we speak, an unconscious deism may already have made considerable headway into the Anglican and other Christian churches without the intentional will of any outside forces. If this is the case, then reason and commonsense have happily already won the day in advance of the deistic proselytising cause.

4 – The resurgent evils of religious terrorism

Deism as a proselytising cause, even when comprised of no more than loosely federated bodies, should refrain from gaining the reputation of a surreptitious movement. Its informal structure, and avoidance of a recognised or elaborate doctrine, naturally helps towards this end, as also does the probability of its wide but unconscious existence in the minds of millions of religious leaders and their followers throughout the globe.

Deists only wish to approach those of every religious persuasion in convincing them that they are *already* deists. This is simply achieved through the easy conversational tone of the Socratic method. Deism is so rational in its procedure and so ethical in its purpose, that mere statements, with hardly a suggestion of argument, are often sufficient to persuade the most difficult prospects. The hammer blows of forceful argument or the subterfuge of circuitous discussion are rarely necessary in promoting deism, since it belongs so clearly to that category known as self-evident truths.

Today we live in a world riven with conflict, and to the surprise of the older generations throughout the industrialised West, it is a bloody conflict arising so obviously from the differences of religion – or at least, through causes which are sublimated through religious factions. In the minds of European peoples, the Wars of religion had exhausted themselves with the horrors of civil bloodshed, torture, and persecution in the 17th century, and religious conflicts since then, further afield, although sometimes ruthless and widespread, had soon burnt themselves out and been forgotten.

Whilst living in Finland in 1968, I remember at a party, being approached by friends and asked, "What's all this about trouble in Ireland?" At the time I had hardly comprehended the events myself which had suddenly broken out in Ulster, but the Finnish papers were filled with the news, and my enlightened friends were dumbstruck by what they had read and seen on their TV screens. "It's unbelievable – it's like the middle ages," they cried in disbelief. "I thought Britain was a civilised place!" exclaimed one aghast. "How is it that Catholics and Protestants can be killing each other?" All I could do in response was try to explain the history of Ireland over the past 300 years, but I soon realised that my lame attempt at an historical exposition was unconvincing. "It's still barbaric. We can't understand it," concluded my friends.

But that was forty years ago. Since then the political situation of the world has been transformed for the worse out of all recognition. Such a dinner party exchange, as described above, would be inconceivable today. Nowhere is there complacency or confidence about the future of humankind! In retrospect the 1960s seems a civilised epoch – even though the Cold War was at the height of its intensity, and the horrors of Vietnam were dragging on from one year to the next. But the outbreak of troubles in Northern Ireland in 1968 did introduce a new element into political life – or at least, resurrected an old element – and it certainly awoke the consciousness to a new kind of political conflict.

Since that time we have witnessed religious conflict and atrocities, on a horrific scale, in many parts of the world, and in the countries of the industrialised West, many live in daily fear for their lives, in the shadow of bomb outrages in shopping centres, on buses, and in underground trains. Religion is very much with us today! In the 1960s the educated and complacent classes may have passed a sigh of relief, under the false impression that the evils and superstition of religion belonged to a forgotten past. Surely the future belonged to the humanistic and civilised values of an agnostic society!

5 – Christian fundamentalism versus that of Islam

The reality, on the contrary, is that the contemporary world is dominated by the forces of religion. Not only is the industrialised West, and the Far East, forced to confront and respond to Islamic fundamentalism, but America, the politically and militarily (if not still economically) most powerful nation on earth, is dominated by statesmen and stateswomen, and industrialists, and opinion-formers, who carry out the "Lord's work" in the name of Christian fundamentalism.

Arab power, collectively worldwide, is puny by comparison with that of America, and so Arabs and all those of other races of the Islamic faith, quite justifiably feel cowed and threatened by the might of Christian aggression. If Christian fundamentalism is intent on arming Israel and promoting the Zionist cause (which it has for eighty years), and if the Christian Right in America is promoting policies for extending the frontiers of Israel, and if Israel is intent on pursuing the policy of dispossessing the Palestinians of their land and property which they have always done, then Christianity may justly be cast in the light of the oppressor of the weak and downtrodden.

These are the natural perceptions held by the Islamic world. Christians are seen as the hypocrites from the privileged affluent West, stamping on the faces of the poor and powerless. But these poor and powerless are not ignorant people without culture or traditions. They have a memory of the past, and many are well educated, and some amongst their number possess wealth beyond belief. All this adds to their resentment, together with the awareness that their values and view of the world differs so greatly from the hated enemy of America.

All this contributes to their feelings of righteousness when resorting to the only means at their disposal in fighting for their personal and ancestral rights. And those means entail the use of the bomb against innocent civilian targets, and if little more is achieved than arousing a global awareness of the situation, then that is sufficient in satisfying a sense of vengeance. The War must continue to be fought by any viable means, for surrender would mean hopelessness and sinking into shameless annihilation. This helps explain the psychology of the Arab mind, and the sympathetic worldwide resurgence of Islamic fundamentalism.

6 – Increasing religiosity accompanies increasing terrorism

The Israeli-Palestinian conflict has worsened conjointly with the increase in religiosity. Until the death of Yasser Arafat, the Palestinian struggle was predominantly secular, but despite the intensity or fanaticism of the PLO (the Palestinian Liberation Organisation), Arafat was always prepared to accept the negotiating offer of new channels for communication. Today the situation is very different. With the victorious election of

Hamas, or the Islamic Resistance Movement (the Arabic acronym of which means "Zeal"), in January 2006 in the Palestinian parliamentary elections, a totally new situation was created.

Hamas was founded in 1987 by Sheikh Ahmed Yassin of the Gaza wing of the Muslim Brotherhood, a fanatical religious body committed to violence in fighting its cause. The Hamas charter formulated in 1988, and still in force, calls for the destruction of the state of Israel and its replacement with a Palestinian Islamic state, covering Israel; the West Bank, and the Gaza Strip, adding that, "There is no solution to the Palestinian question except through Jihad." Since that time, and in the wake of innumerable terrorist outrages, Hamas has been listed as a terrorist organisation by the European Union and many other countries, and is banned in Jordan. In a report issued by Human Rights Watch in 2002, its leader and their activists were declared "accountable for war crimes and crimes against humanity."

Despite these allegations, its current leader, Ismael Haniya Khaled Mashaad, who resides in the safety of Damascus, is seen throughout the Arab world as the most devout and lovable of individuals, and held in the highest regard. On the other hand, all outside channels have broken down as Hamas occupies a pariah status, and so all negotiating routes are blocked in attempts to resolve an on-going situation. What, then, is the next step to be taken? Only the representatives inspired by a neutral religious movement have any hope of breaking the deadlock, and only deism is likely to fulfil such a role. This is because secular movements or secular individuals have little hope of receiving a hearing.

On the wider world stage, it may be seen that the injustice of the Palestinian situation, has acted merely as a catalyst for the spread of religious intolerance and fanaticism, for the followers of the Wahhabi sect in Pakistan, Indonesia, or elsewhere, or the propagandists of Iranian shiism, are only marginally concerned with the Palestinian situation – although the latter have evidently been driven by the American conquest of Iraq. The aggression of Islam towards the industrialised world therefore expresses a general resentment of the weak against the strong, or the sense of righteousness against unrighteousness, rather than a movement against specifically identifiable political or economic wrongs. And this makes, what may be described as the on-going war between the First and Third worlds, so intractable and dangerous.

Nearer at home, in Britain and in many countries of Continental Europe, there is the additional problem of needing to confront the hatred of the West, instilled by Islamic schools within the ruling educational systems of these countries – in addition to the hatred pursued by preaching in the mosques. Such allegations are often the result of hearsay, but occasionally, specific charges reach the public ear. For example, most recently, in February 2007, it was reported that a Moslem convert, Colin Cook, in lodging an unfair dismissal claim with the Watford Employment Tribunal, revealed that the Saudi-funded King Fahad Academy in Acton, West London, was poisoning the minds of those as young as five with a curriculum of hate.

School text books were used which described the Jews as "monkeys" (or apes) and Christians as "pigs," whilst Osama bin Laden was "idolised." The American human rights group, Freedom House, had already identified some of these text books, propagating anti-Western and anti-Semitic views, in a report published in 2006, entitled, *Saudi Arabia's Curriculum of Intolerance*. It is in such schools that Europe's Islamic terrorists of the future are being groomed. It is the kind of religiosity which deism needs to challenge.

7 – The psychological damage of America's fundamentalism

This is the scenario which is presented before the deism of our age. Let us now turn to the problems of Christianity. Christian evangelism is essentially and always priggishly self-righteous (because of its basis in irrationalism, myth, and superstition), and it is aggressive and crusading through its intrinsic nature. Hence the War against "Evil" launched by the Neo-conservative Right is seen as a self-evident necessity and a moral imperative. In the American mind there is no cause for doubting these accepted truths. In such an environment, there are no grounds for compromise and no room for dialogue.

The religious term "fundamentalism" was not first applied to the Saudi sect of Wahhabism, as may be thought by many, but to the Christian Evangelists of America in the 1920s, and something more must be said about the underhand psychological methods and the real evil of Christian fundamentalist theology. In the words of Giles Fraser, an Anglican clergyman and lecturer in philosophy at Wadham College, Oxford, "the key difference between the fundamentalist and non-fundamentalist versions of any world-view, has to do with an ability to accommodate ambiguity and uncertainty. Fundamentalism is a closed system of thought, demanding certainty and providing emotional security. For fundamentalism is commonly an epiphenomenon of change, and has grown in parallel with the rapid social and economic changes that have come about through globalisation. 'Change and decay in all around I see, O thou who changest not, abide with me!'"[24]

Fraser writes, that "the glue of the whole intellectual structure is fear," and that, "Christian fundamentalists inhabit a world of cut-and-dried oppositions: God/world, saved/unsaved, male/female, right/wrong."[25] Chris Hedges, the author of a book on this topic, has written that, "The petrified, binary world of fixed, immutable roles is a world where people, many of them damaged by bouts with failure, can bury their chaotic and fragmented personalities and live with the illusion that they are now strong. Those who do not fit must be proselytised, converted, and 'cured.'"[26] It is surprising and deeply worrying to note that the *Left Behind* series of fundamentalist novels are

---

[24] Giles Fraser, "Blind Faith," *New Statesman*, 5th February 2007, pp. 54-55.
[25] Ibid., p. 55.
[26] Chris Hodges, *American Fascists: The Christian Right & the War on America*, Jonathan Cape, 2007.

now amongst the best selling books in America, and that more than 62 million copies have been printed.

The authors are Jerry Jenkins, a former comic-strip writer, and Tim La Haye, a Southern Baptist minister, and many of the books have been adapted as slasher movies and "Christian" video nasties. The novels propagate the idea that at the end of time God will lift all true Christians into heaven (the so-called "rapture") whilst everybody else is left to fight it out on earth in an orgy of misery and violence. The psychological harm of such teaching in encouraging an introversion and retreat from facing the world of reality is clearly evident, but far more dangerous are the political consequences, when leaders accept and/or encourage such a philosophy, and are guided by such a pessimistic view as to our terrestrial future.

8 – Fortuitous role of the deist as peacemaker

The political role of deism is therefore to break through these walls of intolerance by citing the authority of one who transcends all national, ethnic, religious, or other politically affiliated movements. The subjective conflicts of human groups must be transcended through appealing to a higher authority than the serpentine machinations of quarrelling factions. The adherents of Islam put the concept and worship of God above all other worldly considerations. Indeed, the existence of God is the main topic of conversation of many Arabs when confronted by the "unbeliever," and religious practices remain his chief preoccupation many times during the day for every day of the year.

The deist is placed in an exceptionally advantageous position in winning the ear of the Islamic believer. This is because both the deist and the Moslem believe in the One-God who exists as an omnipotent essence throughout the universe and not as a *personal being* reflecting the image of man. The Islamist would therefore welcome the Westerner professing such a belief, since he has always looked askance at what he perceives as the worshippers of "three gods," two of whom are in "human form." Such a conception of God, in the eyes of the Arab, would remove at once the picture of the *infidel*, and would allow for a friendly welcome and a relaxed discussion on the nature of the Deity over a glass of tea. Of course theological differences would soon be recognised, but as the concept and definition of God overrides all other priorities in the Islamic mind, the deist would already be regarded as having taken the first essential step towards the true faith.

Hence the deist is placed in an exceptional situation as a potential peacemaker. The next task of the intelligent politically negotiating deist is to move away from the topic of religion to the question of justice and disinterested or scientific social ethics, and then onto the practicalities of political decision-making, but frequently returning to the significance of God at every turn of the discussion. By taking such a route he will increasingly gain the confidence and respect of his Islamic friend, for in the Arab world especially, personal relationship between individuals far outweigh the considerations of representative status. That is, the outcome of decision-making in business or politics is not reached according to the perception of an individual's corporate, company, political, or other representative status, but rather according to his characteristics as an ethical or likeable personality in his own right.

Likewise, when the deist finds himself in conversation with the American statesman, or on a lower level of communication, with the evangelising Christian leader, he again has the advantage of confirming his commitment to the belief in God. But beyond that a theological discussion is unlikely to follow or be especially fruitful. Instead the deist should move onto the issue of ethics. Since the American evangelist often supports the principle of predestination, and that the rich and powerful are especially blessed by God, whilst the poor and disadvantaged deserve their lowly status, since God *willed* it that way; and since he believes that the love of money and the grasping after profits are the new Christian virtues which transcend those of the Old World, he should be approached along the lines of, "What kind of a God do you believe in, and how do you define his goodness?" From this, through the Socratic method, the evangelist, through the calm discussion of a step-by-step advance, should be brought to realising the wrongness of his opinions and the injustice of his moral philosophy.

9 – Confused attitude to religion in public life

If deism is to exert any significant impact on the future government of the world, this can only be achieved after it has won great numbers of adherents to the cause who then are prepared to work in a practical way for the future good of humanity and our plant. It is my opinion, if optimism and a better future are to win the day, that the time will arrive when deism is recognised by the majority as the highest form of religion to which all others will be indebted in creating an over-arching religious temperament in uniting all of humankind.

But another more modest and immediate role awaits the fulfilment of deism. In those multicultural societies in Europe and elsewhere, there is confusion, misunderstanding, and doubt about the function of organised religion in public life. How are priorities to be recognised and how is offence to be avoided? How or should tradition be maintained when religious movements from far afield encroach on foreign soil? How is religion to be taught in schools, or what part is it to play during the function of Assemblies? How is religion to be approached by the media in those Christian countries where non-Christian religions begin to dominate. Even when Christianity loses its value as a religious force, it nonetheless retains its cultural significance and loyalty (in a strange way) amongst the majority.

How is one religion to be balanced against another – if indeed, such an idea should be entertained in the first place? Everywhere in Europe anxious steps are taken, as one foot is placed before another, in fear of breaking eggshells. An emphasis is put on teaching comparative religion from the earliest years, and admirable as this is in instilling a spirit of toleration and an interest in foreign customs and beliefs, it achieves little as a preparation for the religious life. No religious belief system is allowed a serious consideration, and when all are given an equal parity, none is allowed a preference above the others.

The cultural outcome in educational terms is therefore the emergence of a kind of pagan view of religious life. In the mind's eye, the images of Christ, Mohammed, and the Buddha may all be erected in the same temple. If religion is to be taught merely as a record of customs and beliefs, or as an inducement to better race relations is it worth teaching in the first place? Such an approach to religion is hardly geared to satisfy the spiritual demands of any faith. Would it not therefore be preferable to teach some other aspect of human knowledge, as for example, philosophy or science?

The above illustrates our contemporary dilemma with regard to our attitude to religion, and as to the role it should play in school education. The causes for this stem from the agnostic or irreligious age in which we live. But because we are tied to the legacy of our origins, educationalists are forced to adopt a confused and hypocritical approach to a religion which is torn away from the concept of belief. And this messy compromising attitude leads to an embarrassment for all – for teachers and pupils alike. As religion is a deeply serious matter, it should be treated as such, but in the present climate of opinion, the difficulties are too great in teaching the subject as it properly deserves.

10 – A role for deism in public life

There is only one way out of all these difficulties. Only deism as a religious belief system, retains sufficient credibility in the minds of the majority, to secure its function as a spiritually uplifting influence in society. Its non-divisive, all-inclusive, and over-arching characteristics, puts it in the position of a neutral religious role, acceptable to all faiths and sects of goodwill. It is therefore proposed in this book that deism, in possessing the minimum essentials for a monotheistic faith, should be adopted in all spheres of public life where religious formality is required, e.g., with regard to the swearing of oaths or solemn promises, etc. It should be noted, in parenthesis, that most polytheistic faiths also comprise the monotheistic characteristic of recognising a leading God, or a unified essence expressed as a Supreme Being.

In our multicultural society it would therefore be advantageous to all, if schools were obliged to recognise the religion of Deism in embracing and expressing the good ethical will of all faiths worldwide. This is because deism is the religion of respect and understanding. If deism was adopted for practice in public life, much embarrassment, hypocrisy, misunderstanding, and offence would be avoided in so many social situations. If deism was granted such a discreet function in public life, I believe it would exalt rather than diminish the influence of the established churches.

There are two reasons for this: firstly, because the state would grant recognition to the Godhead in the abstract acceptable to all sectors of society; and secondly, because many who are currently agnostic or atheistic and yet necessarily involved in religious formalities (e.g. especially those in the teaching profession) would be drawn into a religious frame of mind through the attractions of deism. Today we live in a world of religion versus agnosticism and atheism, and such a sharp duality would be greatly diminished if the latter were substituted in favour of deism. The rational basis of deism together with its ethical appeal, I believe, is capable of sidelining or removing the non-religious outlook which preponderates in contemporary society.

11 – A Moral Rearmament for social progress

There is, perhaps, a social role for deism which transcends all others, and that is in the creation of a new moral consciousness in the sphere of political activity. A watershed has now been reached with regard to the future path in promoting justice and equity for the peoples of the world. Shortly after the collapse of the East bloc in 1989, the Neo-Conservative (or Neo-Liberal) American intelligentsia were quick to fill the gap in claiming that they alone pointed the way ahead, through promoting unrestricted corporate global capitalism. No other ideology stood in their way. The ills of such a path are too numerous and too obvious to repeat in a book of this nature.

Meanwhile, world Socialism has become totally discredited: for whilst in China the Communist Party had already created an ambiguous situation by calling for a "get rich first" policy, in summoning free market capitalism into existence alongside a state regulated market, which presages problems for the future; the Western parliamentary parties of the left, following in the wake of New Zealand in 1987,[27] began dismantling the safety net of the welfare services established in the post-War period. This surrender to the policies of Thatcherism has occurred partly through the sheer power of international American-style capitalism, and partly through the dismal failure of Socialists worldwide to discriminate knowledgeably between the benign and malign aspects of different capitalistic system.

It is probable that Socialism may never again be regenerated because of the consequences of the total transformation of the structure of society over the past six decades throughout the industrialised world. Socialism was ever dependent on the revolutionary ethos, which in the more democratic economies was minimised down to a covert, albeit, a militant class-consciousness, but evoking such an ethos in today's society (however so minimised) is increasingly difficult. This is simply because we now live in a heterogeneous society of the middle-middle majority, sharing common economic and other political anxieties, and no longer in a world divided by a distinctive and visible bourgeoisie versus a resentful proletariat.

This means that the left/right political divisions, which have haunted society since 1789, are no longer viable as a

---

[27]   With the free market "Rogernomics" of the Labour leader, Roger Douglas.

democratic means in pushing forward the needs or progress of society. This has therefore created an unusual and interesting situation. There are no longer in the industrialised world powerful parliamentary movements effectively (or in actuality) promoting the interests of the less powerful in society. This means, in effect, that there are no political movements to confront the ubiquity of the transnational corporations. In practice, we are now finding that the parliamentary parties of the right are now beginning to represent the weaker and more disadvantageous sectors of the community, since they have little to lose and much to gain from such an ideological shift in responding to the needs of a heterogeneous middle-middle majority whose economic and social interests do not allow for the old divisions of the past. Nonetheless, that minority comprising the active political classes of every hue, now find themselves in an ideological limbo, and because of their lifelong loyalties, they can hardly acknowledge the changes which have occurred.

It is into such a vacuum that deism may bring to bear its social ethics. As a religious rather than a political movement, it may stand aside from party preference, whilst encouraging those parliamentary or other groups promoting the disinterested cause of social justice and an upwardly-aspiring egalitarianism, as described in my earlier book, *Populism Against Progress*. Such a campaign for social justice may be launched as a Moral Rearmament addressed not merely to the world of politics, but to the Churches and the broad mass of society and all thoughtful people of goodwill irrespective of their status or background. In this way deism may be firmly established in the public eye as an ethical movement for social progress.

Religion, as we have argued, is a natural component of humankind and is therefore ineradicable. If it is to exist as a healthy influence, it would preferably evolve in conjunction with human progress, but in any event it will continue in one form or another for good or ill. Surely, therefore, the most ardent non-believers must recognise the value of deism as a useful inoculation against the more harmful aspects of organised religion, or in a predominantly secular society, against the emergence of pseudo-religious or pagan movements as nature worship, astrology, divination of some kind, animism, or mystic belief in the power of special objects or places. The promoters of atheism are therefore unrealistic in both their understanding and expectations of human nature when they predict the demise of religion. They may indeed be justified in their critique of religion as they find it, but that alone cannot justify their argument for the dissolution of religion.

It would be more realistic if they argued for its transformation towards a deistic direction, and I believe that in the latter, even the most ardent atheists would find few grounds for objection. This book has been written as an answer to Richard Dawkins best seller, *The God Delusion*. The present book is not so much intended as a refutation of Dawkins, for he is always reasonable and usually aims his shafts in the right direction, but there are gaps in his thinking which leave huge questions to be answered about the embedded spiritual needs of humankind inherent in his nature. And this book is an attempt to answer some of these questions.

CHAPTER 4

THE LEGACY OF DEISM

"The early rise of deism in all countries was strongly abetted by the growth of the spirit of toleration, and deism, in its turn, has strongly contributed to the continued growth and acceptance of toleration of other views. Perhaps, in the most universal sense, this is the major legacy of historical deism to the modern world."

The Encyclopedia of Philosophy, Macmillan & Free Press, NY, 1967, Vol. II, p. 335.

1 – How deism is absurdly misapprehended

Deism is one of the greatest unsung (even little known) glories in the history of English thought, and because of the widespread ignorance and misunderstanding of deism – even in academic circles – something must be said about its origin and early history.

It has been falsely described as never having been "widely accepted in England," (e.g. the *Oxford English Dictionary*), when in fact deism originated and first flourished as a powerful movement in England, from where it spread with even greater influence to Europe and across the Atlantic to the American colonies. Deism has been confusingly described as advancing the idea of the "absentee God," or as a God who set up the mechanism of the universe before mysteriously disappearing into retirement. The perplexities and absurdities surrounding the perceptions of deism, because they are so often repeated in supposedly-informed books and works of reference, originate in all possibility from the tradition of discrediting its existence, rather than from serious attempts to elucidate its proper significance.

The great age of English deism, during which a mass of literature was produced, extends roughly between 1680-1740. The greatest or most well known deistic works, however, were produced some four decades after this later date, viz., Paine's the *Age of Reason* (1794-96), and Kant's, *Religion Within The Limits of Reason Alone* (1794), and although the second half of the 18th century produced many works influenced by deistic thinking, usually by enlightened members of the clergy (e.g. Dr. Hugh Blair), the great age of deism was over before the accession of George III in 1760. We shall explain the reasons below not only for the sudden demise of deism as an intellectual movement, but for its intentional burial beneath a mound of forgetfulness. One explicable reason for the ignorance of deism today is that it sits uncomfortably between the stools of Religion and Philosophy, and consequently it receives little attention from either of these bodies of knowledge in their works of learning.

An attempt to disentangle the antecedents of historical deism – intertwined as they are with rationalistic natural religion on the one hand, and scepticism on the other – would be a difficult and fruitless task. From early in the 16th century deism was associated with anti-Trinitarianism, Unitarianism, secularism, anticlericalism, Erastianism, Arminianism, Socinianism, and religious toleration generally. John Dryden in the Preface to his poem *Religio Laici* (1682) equated deism with "natural religion."

2 – Early history of deism

Lord Herbert of Cherbury (1583-1648) is regarded as the founding proponent of deism although he never described himself as a deist. In his *De Veritate, Prout Distinguitur a Revelatione, a Verisimile, a Possibili, et a false* (*On Truth, as it is distinguished from Revelation, the Probable, the Possible, and the false*), published in Paris in 1624 and then in London in 1633 and 1645, he laid down the rationalistic basis of deism which was to be assumed, if not always acknowledged, by virtually all succeeding deists in the years ahead. In the third edition of this work which appeared in London in 1645, to which he added a short treatise, *De Causis Errorum*, a dissertation entitled, *Religio Laici*, and an *Appendix ad*

Sacerdotes, he enumerates what he perceives as the five guiding principles of deism, as: Firstly, that there is one Supreme God; Secondly, that he ought to be worshipped; Thirdly, that virtue and piety are the chief parts of divine worship; Fourthly, that man ought to be sorry for his sins and repent of them, and Fifthly, that divine goodness dispenses rewards and punishments both in this life and after it. These truths, he argued, are universal and may be apprehended by reason.

His *De Religione Gentilium,* appeared posthumously in 1663, which is a treatise on comparative religion, and a popular account of his views on religion was published in 1768 under the title of, *A Dialogue between a Tutor and his Pupil, by Edward Lord Herbert of Chirbury*, but the evidence is uncertain as to whether this work is entirely from his pen.

During the Commonwealth, the deists seem to have attracted the enmity of Cromwell, and after having overthrown the Republicans, he was then confronted by the Independents who divided between the millenarians and the deists. Hume, writing of the period around 1653, records that the deists, "had no other object than political liberty, who denied entirely the truth of revelation, and insinuated that all the various sects, so heated against each other, were alike founded on folly and in error. Men of such daring geniuses were not contented with the ancient and legal forms of civil government, but challenged a degree of freedom beyond what they expected ever to enjoy under any monarchy. Martin, Challoner, Harrington, Sidney, Wildman, Nevil, were esteemed the heads of this small division. The deists were perfectly hated by Cromwell, because he had no hold of enthusiasm, by which he could govern or over-reach them; he therefore treated them with great rigour and disdain, and usually denominated them the heathens."[28]

In the second half of the 17th century, deism was propagated (sometimes perhaps surreptitiously) through humanism in general, e.g., as seen in the philosophy of Hobbes; the idealism of James Harrington; in the natural Biblical

---

[28]   David Hume, *History of England*, printed for Richardson & Co., etc., 1820 ed., Vol. III, pp. 226-227 (Chapter 61).

exegesis of Spinoza and others; in the widespread religions rationalism of the Cambridge Platonists and other Latitudinarians; the "sweet reasonableness" of Locke; and the scientific approach of Newton.

It is interesting to trace the earliest use of the term deism, and how by various steps it eventually came to be noticed as a significant concept to be developed and propagated by English thinkers early in the 18th century. The first known use of the term deist was by Pierre Viret, a disciple of Calvin, in his *Instruction Chrétienne*, Geneva, 1564, in an "Epistre" signed in Lyons on 12th December 1563. Viret regarded it as an entirely new word which he claimed the deists wished to put in opposition to "atheism" in avoiding the accusation of the latter. According to Viret, deists profess belief in God as the creator of heaven and earth, but reject Jesus Christ and his doctrines. Although these unidentified deists were acknowledged as learned men of letters and philosophy, they were bitterly attacked by Viret as "monsters and atheists."

The above definition and commentary was lifted from its original source more than a century later and published in Pierre Bayle's remarkable encyclopaedia of philosophical and religious scepticism, the *Dictionaire historique et critique*, which was to exert a widespread influence throughout Europe in the 18th century. The work was published in the safety of the Netherlands in 1697, and an English translation of this massive work appeared in 1710, and it soon regenerated the existing interest and debate on deism.[29]

3 – The great age of English Deism

The great age of overt deism may be dated from 1679 with the publication of Charles Blount's (1654-1693) *Anima Mundi*, a defence of the system of natural religion incorporating an appreciation of the comparative merits of the pagan religions.

---

[29]   It should be noted that the word deism first appeared in print in England in Robert Burton's, *The Anatomy of Melancholy* (1621), III iv, II i. After discussing atheists and near-atheists, Burton continues, "Cousin-germans to these men are many of our great Philosophers and Deists," who although good and moral are yet themselves atheists.

This was followed by, *Diana of the Ephesians* (1680), an attack on priestcraft, and a *Summary Account of The Deists' Religion*, which appeared posthumously in 1693. Three years later, John Toland (1670-1722) published his, *Christianity not mysterious: or a Treatuse shewing That there is nothing in the Gospel contrary to Reason, nor above; And that no Christian Doctrine can properly be call'd a Mystery.* This book, which is rationalistic and reminiscent of Herbert's *De Veritate*, opposes not only Biblical mysteries but also challenges the validity of the Biblical canon and identifies corruptions in Biblical texts. Toland mocks the implicit faith of the Puritans and their bibliolatry, and censures the vested interests of priests of all denominations. Toland was in the tradition of Bruno, Descartes, Spinoza, and Leibnitz, and to a lesser extent, to Locke, and his learning brought him international renown.

By the start of the 18th century deism was already recognised as an active intellectual movement, and so the rationalist Anglican theologian, Samuel Clarke (a prominent opponent of deism), in 1704 was able to distinguish the four varieties of deists (as he saw them) as, firstly, Those who denied providence; secondly, Those who acknowledged providence in natural religion, but not in morality; thirdly, Those who, while denying a future life, admitted the moral role of the deity; and fourthly, Those who acknowledged a future life and the other doctrines of natural religion.

Anthony Collins (1676-1729) was the most readable and urbane of all the English deists, and he is notable for the fact that he regarded "enthusiasm" (that great 18th century term for fanaticism) and superstition as evils which were greater than atheism. Amongst his leading works are, *An Essay Concerning the Use of Reason* (1707), *Priestcraft in Perfection* (1709), and his most famous book, *Discourse of Free-Thinking* (1713).

The most learned of British deists, as well as the most significant historically, was Matthew Tindal (c1657-1733), author of *Christianity as Old as Creation; or the Gospel A Republication of the Religion of Nature* (1730). This work was at once recognised as "The deist's Bible." He argues that

Scripture, replete with ambiguities, is not only unnecessary but is actually confusing to men of reason, and all men (and women) of whatever education or status in life are capable of Right Reason.

Another prominent thinker was William Wollaston (1660-1724), whose works were widely read and well received. His *Religion of Nature Delineated* (1724) was subsequently applaued by Queen Caroline "the Illustrious," consort of George II. He argues that man knows the truth by means of reason, and that it is his duty to seek happiness, or the excess of pleasure over pain, since that is essentially part of man's approach to truth. The book is free of Biblical criticism and is entirely rationalistic. Thomas Woolston (1670-1731), a disciple of Anthony Collins, was not so fortunate in his endeavours. He spearheaded the assault on Biblical prophecies, extending the attack to that on Biblical miracles. His *Discourses on the Miracles of Our Saviour, In view of the Present contest between Infidels and Apostates* (1727-1729), called upon his head the ire of the authorities, for he was prosecuted and convicted for blasphemy, being fined £100 plus a year in prison, where he died in 1731 unable to pay the fine.[30]

It may be gauged from the above that the British deists constituted no conspiracy, and no distinctive school of thought, were highly individualistic, and often unknown to one another. It is also remarkable and shameful that in view of the huge amount of deistic literature, and the outstanding scholarship it produced overall in England between 1680-1740, that, firstly, so little is known about these authors and their writings; and secondly, that if the researcher wishes to undertake serious study of their works, he is usually obliged to consult the efforts of German scholars in his quest, such as G.V. Lechler's, *Geschichte des englischen Deismus,* Stuttgart, 1841, or, Ludwig Noack's 3-volume work, *Die Freidenker in der Religion* (1853-1855). This is partly because English deism is held in greater regard on the Continent and elsewhere, and partly because of

---

[30] See Appendix for a list of the most prominent English works during the great age of British deism.

the broader interest in intellectual movements generally which is to be found there.

4 – Deism coincided with a high point in British civilisation

It should be appreciated that the period between the Glorious Revolution in 1688-89 and 1740, marked a significant high point in British civilisation expressed in terms of well-balanced intellectual values and a newly awakened social consciousness with regard to good government and truthful thinking. This led in turn to the consideration of civilised manners and attitudes, and the cultivation of polite conversation as an art in raising the quality of social life.

This thinking and way of life emerged as a reaction against the previous two centuries of intolerance and religious wars, which had torn Europe apart in a needless catalogue of civil bloodshed and horrors. And religion had been the cause and the evil for all that had passed. With the Protestant Settlement in 1688, and the final end of monarchical absolutism, the new era looked forward with optimism to an age of reason, freed from the fanaticism of the past. The well-balanced values of the 18th century may be defined as not only rational and psychologically sound in their freedom from hidden pathological repressions, but also profoundly ethical.

The spirit of the age was most clearly expressed through the urbanity of the *Spectator*, which appeared several times weekly between 1711-1714. This journal which attracted the most diverse talents of the age, including Addison, Steele, Pope, and Swift, forbad articles touching on the topics of religion or politics, whilst encouraging contributions discussing the manners, fashions, or foibles of the age; or humorous observations of life, stories with a moral point, light philosophical digressions and essays on sundry subjects – or anything which contributed to the civilising or improvement of everyday life. The literary experimentation of the *Spectator* led inevitably to the development of the novel and eventually to the masterpieces of Richardson, Fielding, and Smollett.

It was an age, before the rise of a modern national consciousness, when the informed classes were far more international in their outlook than today. The obligatory Grand Tour of several years, ensured that the educated gentleman of good repute – and many with limited financial means were included amongst the number[31] - was as much at home in society in Paris, Rome, Vienna, and cities surrounding the major courts of Germany, as he was in his native London. And if he failed to achieve a fluency in all the leading West European tongues, he was always able to revert to Latin in cementing life-long friendships and understanding. It should be added that by comparison the so-called educated classes of today are provincial, narrow-minded, and moronic.

It was into this fortuitous intellectual climate that deism was born and flourished as the religion of reason and sanity. If progress is perceived as a lineal development (which unfortunately in reality it is not) it would be anticipated that in such a climate deism would triumph as an ongoing intellectual force, which if not actually supplanting the established churches, would at least exist alongside them as a significant religious influence. But this was not to be. Instead, deism was not merely to disappear, but to be buried in a grave of forgetfulness.

It is now our task to investigate how exactly this occurred. In the general debate on deism, by secular and religious thinkers alike, the rationalistic refutations were prolific and formidable. But the rationalistic approach achieved little in defeating the deist cause, for the ironic reason that its opponents were so similar in their modes of thinking.

5 – Causes for the demise of English deism

The forces which were eventually to dissolve the English deism of the 18th century arose from causes which were not only different but in opposition to one another. The first arose,

---

[31] Thomas Gray, the poet, and the Irish writer, Oliver Goldsmith, to name several. The indigent middle classes on the grand tour were often in the company of well-to-do patrons and members of the nobility, whom they sometimes served as scholarly cicerones.

surprisingly, from the arguments of David Hume, who set out to undermine the vulnerable a priori basis of deism, although more recent scholarship tends to discredit this commonly held assumption. The objection of contemporary scholars is based on three grounds: firstly, that deism was already in rapid decline on the publication of those works relevant to the criticism of deism; secondly, that Hume's writings on religion exerted little influence at the time of their publication; and thirdly, that Hume's scepticism about the validity of natural religion cuts equally against deism and those opponents of deism who were also deeply involved in natural theology.

Nonetheless, in retrospect, Hume's critique of deism remains interesting and significant. His most important work in this context is perhaps his, *Dialogues Concerning Natural Religion*, published posthumously in 1779. More interesting, though, is his earlier work, *The Natural History of Religion* (1757) which demonstrated that polytheism and not monotheism was the first and must ancient religion of humankind, and that the psychological basis of religion is not reason but fear of the unknown. Deists are unlikely to quarrel with such conclusions.

Hume was the universal sceptic, and may be described as a gentle atheist, and in this may be traced his emotional response to the existence of deism. He was the first of many atheists up until the present time who have attempted to drive their barbs into the truths of the deist cause. And such a futile activity, it may be observed, is perhaps more motivated by an insistence on driving away any lingering doubts about the remaining truths of religion, or even by intellectual vanity, than by the feelings of the heart or the search for truth. Hume was amongst the most equable and inoffensive of personalities, but his empirical philosophy was driven by an ice-cold rationalism, and since he flourished some two hundred years before there developed a psychoanalytic analysis of the mind, it may be suggested that perhaps he was denied the necessary opportunity for appreciating the human or social need for religion.

Hume was in Paris on a diplomatic mission in 1746, and Secretary to the ambassador for France between 1763-65, where he was lionised by the Court and literary society, but he was shocked by the mutation of deism into a militant atheism, as expressed by such thinkers as d'Alembert and Diderot (both editors of the famous *Encyclopédie*), and Baron d'Holbach, La Mettrie, Grimm, Condillac, Condorcet, and other *philosophes* – and it may be noted that the sceptical Gibbon had reservations on this matter as those of Hume. It may therefore be surmised that Hume was not averse to perceiving deism as somehow blameworthy for a socially undesirable or distasteful atheism, and that this may also have offended his Tory sensibilities.

But the deism which emerged in France by the middle of the 18th century was different from that which had earlier flourished in England, and English deism never did mutate into militant atheism. The political and intellectual climate was quite different in France, where a hugely wealthy, corrupt, and powerful church imposed a tyrannical authority over a cowed and economically hard-pressed people. Hence the reactions of such a people were understandably too ready to challenge the demands of religion in any guise it existed in tearing it apart.

The second cause which brought about the demise of English deism is far more significant and comprehensible. This was the influence of emotionalism and "enthusiasm" which finally triumphed in reviving the old-established religious beliefs. William Law (1688-1761) and Bishop Joseph Butler (1692-1752) led the anti-rationalistic assaults on deism, the former through faith, the latter through matter of fact.

But far more powerful still, was the clever evangelising work of John Wesley (1703-1791), with his open air mass rallies and use of crowd psychology. Through appealing to "enthusiasm," he propagated the doctrine of continuous personal inspiration and the inner conversation of the soul: "By grace are ye saved through faith!" We shall turn again to the underhand methods of Wesley in Chapter 9 of this book.

6 – War and its destruction of rational ideals

By the end of the 18th century deism in England had all but melted away. A new intellectual environment and new feelings had emerged in the wake of revolution, ideological war, and the raising of conscript armies which had been unknown in the former era. Rationalism belonged to a past epoch, and when the age of reason had gone, Britain lost something of her sound psychological balance.

Emotionalism and morbid obsessions had taken over the calm and peace of the undisturbed soul. This sickness was reflected through the excesses of romanticism, the absurdities of the Gothic novel, effusive sentimentality, and in the sphere of religion, later in the following century, by the Oxford movement, and a church which not only returned to the middle ages, but from then onward anticipated that all churches should be built in the dark gothic style – contrasting so sharply with the light and careful proportions of the classical or English Renaissance temples of worship which had preceded them.

All this morbidity, and yearning for a lost past, offers of course, a rich pasture for the psychiatrist. The age of reason, on the contrary, presented the image of humankind in as sane and agreeable a character in his *intellectual mindset* as he is ever likely to be portrayed in our long-suffering planet. In 1790, Edmund Burke smugly exclaimed, "Who born within the last forty years has read one word of Collins and Toland, and Tindal and Chubb, and Morgan, and that whole race who called themselves freethinkers? Who now reads Bolingbroke? Who ever read him through?"

But Burke had spoken too readily. The deist flame had not entirely been extinguished in his adopted land. In the early 19th century radical publishers as William Benbow, William Hone, and most notably Richard Carlile (1790-1843), all of whom were political as well as religious reformers, flooded the market with such periodicals as, *The Deist or Moral Philosopher* (1819-20), and pamphlets and cheap reprints from an earlier and wiser era.

It is significant, however, that following the appearance of Burke's *Reflections on the French Revolution* (1790), and even more so with the appearance of his, *Appeal from the New to the Old Whigs*, and, *Thoughts on French Affairs* (both in 1791), and his hysterical, *Letters on a Regicide Peace* (1796-97), all calling for upholding tradition in all its aspects, and the latter urging the government to suppress free opinion at home; radical, Utilitarian, and most rational thinkers with advanced views, were almost forced into an underground existence.

Enlightened men of the stamp of Godwin, Priestley (whose house was ransacked by the mob for his response to Burke's *Reflections*), Bentham, Blake (who had his brush with the law arising from an alleged insult in reference to the War – a charge for which he was triumphantly acquitted), and somewhat later, James Mill, Joseph Hume, and their circle, were never truly successful in gaining the hearing they deserved. All either wavered between or adhered to the principles of Unitarianism, deism, or atheism.

The tragedy of their failure in advancing their ideas is accountable to the fact that war is always a coarse and corrosive influence on the constructive intellectual life of a nation, and the outcome of the Napoleonic Wars was the final assault on the Enlightenment and rational thought. And ideologically motivated wars are the worst of all in destroying intellectual life, or in giving rise to an inauspicious intellectual climate, which encourages falsehood and the poison of deep-seated and lingering hatred. And the Napoleonic Wars were the first ideological conflicts in modern history to tear the world apart.

The above historical elucidation of the circumstances describing the demise of 18th century deism in Britain is not intended as a hymn to a past age, or a return to an earlier epoch, but only an appeal to regenerating the intellectual rationalism of the 18th century, and setting it within the modern framework of our own time.

7 – English deism in France and Germany

A more encouraging picture is presented as soon as we turn to considering the influence of English deism abroad. Both Voltaire and Montesquieu visited England early in the 18th century,[32] and were entranced by the freedom they encountered, the success of our parliamentary traditions, the justice of our laws and the excellence of the legal system, and the general prosperity of ordinary people in that pre-industrial age. They mixed in high circles and applied themselves with diligence in studying the writings of the current thinkers, poets, and other men and women who had made their literary mark.

During his 3-year stay in England, Voltaire was introduced by his friend, Bolingbroke, to Alexander Pope and his circle, and he then became acquainted with Peterborough, Chesterfield, the Herveys, the Duchess of Marlborough, and the poets, Edward Young, James Thomson, and John Gray. Under the influence of these French visitors, deism achieved a renewed vigour in France, although as we have said, it sometimes mutated into militant atheism.

It is also interesting to note that, in the words of Robertson, Voltaire "was already something of a freethinker when a mere child. So common was deism already become in France at the end of the 17th century that his godfather, an abbé, is said to have taught him, at the age of three, a poem by J.B. Rouseau,[33] then privately circulated, in which Moses in particular and religious revelations in general are derided as fraudulent. Knowing this poem by heart in his childhood, the boy was well on the way to his life's work. It is on records that many of his school-fellows were, like himself, already deists."[34]

The deism of Voltaire is reflected throughout his works, in plays and novella, as well as in letters, essays and treatises. His conviction was that if God did not exist, it would be necessary to invent him, a sentiment he repeated in a letter to Frederick the Great in 1770. And this conviction fits nicely with the

---

[32] Voltaire in 1726-29 and Montesquieu in 1729-31.
[33] No relative of J.J. Rouseau.
[34] J.M. Robertson, op. cit., Vol. II, p. 215.

contemporary view of psychology in explaining the need for religion even in an enlightened world. His deism is perhaps best summarised in his, *Traité sur la Tolérance* (1763); the *Dictionaire philosophique* (1764); and the earlier, *Lettres philosophique* (1734) which was burnt by the common hangman. In the latter work he eulogises the Quakers as ideal deists for their freedom of thought and freedom from dogmatism and clericalism. A different but equally admirable deism is reflected in Rousseau's, *Émile, ou de l'education* (1762).

After 1740, on the accession of the first modern freethinking king, Frederick the Great of Prussia, numerous translations of the English deists and their orthodox refuters were published, as indicated in G.W. Alberti's, *Briefe betreffend den allerneusten Zustand der Religion und der Wissenschaften in Gross-Brittanien* (1752-54). Enlightened Prussia was a refuge for the persecuted of all faiths, and French Huguenots flocked to Berlin following the Revocation of the Edict of Nantes in 1685, and the French baroque Cathedral which stands in the centre of that city to this day (and recently, newly restored), is a witness to the welcome given to these persecuted people.

Frederick famously declared that, "All religions must be tolerated ... for in this country every man must get to heaven in his own way." These words were originally scribbled in the margin of a report concerning Roman Catholic Schools on 22nd June 1740. Carlyle in his masterly biography of "Old Fritz", gives a full account of these circumstances, and after commenting on the King's poor German spelling and grammatical errors,[35] he continues in his inimitable style, "Wonderful words; precious to the then leading spirits and which (the spelling and grammar being mended) flew abroad over all the world; the enlightened Public everywhere answering

---

[35] Frederick, of course, spoke French on an every day basis, a language in which he had some literary pretensions to poetry, which behind his back, gained the derision of his friend Voltaire. In this age before the rise of national consciousness, the King was able to insist that he "only spoke German to his dog."

his Majesty, once more, with its loudest 'Bravissimo!' on this occasion."[36]

The German deists were called *Freidenkers* (Freethinkers) and amongst their most prominent leaders were: Herrmann Samuel Reimarus (1694-1768); Johann Christian Edelmann (1698-1767); Moses Mendelssohn (1729-1786) who lived entirely in the sphere of deism and natural religion, and sought to give religion an ethical structure; Gotthold Ephraim Lessing (1729-1781), a close friend of Mendelsshon, a prominent Judophile, and an outstanding figure in the history of Biblical criticism and an unbeliever from student days; Christoph Martin Wieland (1733-1813) who was strongly influenced by Shaftesbury, and wrote on the free use of reason in matters of faith; Johann Eberhard (1739-1809) a prolific writer and author of the 2-volume works, *Neue Apologie des Socrates*; and Karl Friedrich Bahrdt (1741-1792) a once orthodox theologian who towards the latter part of his life repudiated the accepted doctrines and lectured widely on a new "moral system" for replacing supernatural Christianity.

Other works produced during the same period were, J.A. Trinius' *Freydenker-Lexicon* (1759), and, U.G. Thorschmid's *Freidenker-Bibliothek* (1765-67). In demonstrating the lively cross-fertilisation of ideas, in 1766, Reimarus's book originally published in 1755, *The Principal Truths of Natural Religion Defended and Illustrated*, was translated and presented to English readers.

Until the death of Frederich the Great in 1784, after which a reaction set in with the accession of his nephew, Frederick William II, to re-establish the old religious orthodoxies, Berlin remained a leading intellectual centre of the Enlightenment. The extent of this was so marked that following the public observation of a leading German preacher in 1777, the term "Berliner" quickly became a synonym for a "Rationalist."

Kant's book, referred to in an earlier chapter, *Religion Within the Limits of Reason Alone*, appeared much later in

[36] Thomas Carlyle, *History of Friedrich II of Prussia*, Chapman Hall, 1862, Vol. III, pp. 16-17.

1792-94. The approach is basically naturalistic, and religion is set within the boundaries of conscience or practical works. Christianity is stripped of its mystery, and tradition is regarded in a purely moral light. God is conceived as the moral creator of the world, and on those grounds it is the duty of good men to worship him.

8 – English deism in America

English deism exerted its most widespread influence in the American colonies, and the majority of leading thinkers and founders of the United States, seem to have adopted deistic ideas but regretfully in a somewhat covert fashion in deferring to the established forms of Christianity. Benjamin Franklin (1706-1790) acknowledged himself to intimate friends as a deist as early as 1723, but nonetheless continued a lifelong church attendance, thereby setting the conservative pattern followed by most of the leaders in the Colonial and Revolutionary periods.

Thomas Jefferson (1743-1826), although a member of the Episcopal Church, was in reality a deist, rationalist, and above all, a humanitarian. He compiled but never published what later became known as, *The Jefferson Bible, being The Life and Morals of Jesus Christ of Nazareth*. This little work, comprising a cento of clippings from the Gospels of Matthew, Mark, Luke and John, posted in a blank book, extols Jesus as a man for his moral teachings, omits ambiguous and controversial passages, and while rejecting many of the supernatural elements, presents the core of Christian morality and is genuinely religious in tone. Hence religion for both Franklin and Jefferson was essentially a utilitarian moral code.

George Washington was also a deist, although he always maintained a church pew, but he insisted on a total separation between church and state, and ensured that no reference to Christianity or even the Deity was made in the Constitution. In answer to a direct question from a Muslim potentate in Tripoli, he acquiesced in the declaration of Joel Barlow, the American

Consul in Algiers, that "the Government of the United States of America is not in any sense founded on the Christian religion."

Other prominent founding fathers who were deists were, John Quincey Adams, James Madison, Cornelius Harnett, Gouverneur Morris, Hugh Williamson, and James Wilson. In Harvard in 1755 the Dudleian Lectures were established for the purpose of explicating natural religion, but the major deistic publications of America did not appear until late in the century. Notable was Ethan Allen's (1738-1789), *Reason the Only Oracle of Man, or a Compendious system of Natural Religion* (1784), influenced by the earlier British deists; and, Elihu Palmer's (1764-1806), *Principles of Nature, or a Development of the Moral Causes of Happiness and Misery among the Human Species* (1794), being an early defence of the First Book of Paine's, *Age of Reason*. Between 1803-05 Palmer edited the deistical paper, *Prospect; or View of the Moral World*, and he also organised the Deistical Society in New York. Philip Freneau (1752-1832), meanwhile, belonged to a very rare species, being a deistic poet, the author of such poems as, *Belief and Unbelief: Humbly recommended to the serious consideration of Creed Makers, Uniformity and Perfection of Nature*, and, *On the Religion of Nature*.

It is a supreme irony, that now in the 21st century, we find an American government and an intellectual establishment behind American world power, which has retrogressed from the enlightened rationalism of the 18th century, to a primitive religiosity more worthy of the middle ages. Over the same period America may have advanced economically and industrially, but in terms of true religion and ethical values, she has moved in the opposite direction. Only through reversing such a trend and returning to her deistic roots, can she hope to recover her moral greatness in the eyes of the world.

Thomas Paine, who ended his career and life in America, was not overtly a deist until the publication of his, *The Age of Reason: Being an Investigation of True and Fabulous Theology* (1794-96). The First Book sought to rescue deism from the then dominating French atheism, and is a scientific assault on revealed religion in general as being supererogatory to natural religion. This was accepted without too much controversy by the enlightened elite, but the Second Book, published a year later, attacked both the Old and New Testaments, arguing that the Bible was not the Word of God and depicting Christianity as a species of atheism.

This offended readers in American and England, as well as in France, and ironically, in view of the status which the book maintains today, it led to the personal ruin of Paine, through the alienation of his friends, social ostracism as an atheist, poverty, and death in obscurity. But worse still, it led to the denigration and fall of deism as a movement with lasting influence. In America this occurred, on the one hand, through its submergence by evangelism amongst the semiliterate masses; and on the other hand, by its absorption by Unitarianism amongst the better educated.

Having elaborated on the principles for regenerating a new deism for the third millennium, and having given a survey of deism during the period of its greatest success, the following ten chapters present a deistic perspective of religion and the different churches worldwide as we find them both historically and today. The last two chapters then return to formulating a deistic approach to several important aspects of religion.

CHAPTER 5
The Corner-Stone of Religion

"Religion is the great dynamic force in social life, and the vital changes in civilization are always linked with the changes in religious beliefs and ideals."

Christopher Dawson, *Progress & Religion*, Sheed Ward, 1929, p. 234.

1 – Ethics as the corner-stone of religion

The purpose of religion has always been perceived as representing the highest authority over the individual and society in the striving of life along the path of ultimate values. That is why the administration of oaths, and the most important events in the life of the individual, viz., birth, marriage and death, are given a religious dimension in underlining the values of their significance.

This all-important factor means that the question of religion should be approached with the deepest sincerity, and sincerity should be linked to the demands of disinterested truth. This is because the first concern of religion, in the eyes of the ordinary person, is with righteousness, and righteousness cannot be separated from a rigorous understanding of the truth in the light of all reasonable scepticism.

This means that religion in the eyes of the ordinary person – even in those of the non-believer – is, or should be, concerned with ultimate values of an ethical nature. Indeed, if religion is not concerned with ultimate ethical values, it is perceived as worthless. The sole remaining link of sympathy between the agnostic and the cause of religion is the belief that the latter purports – or strives to be the final guardian of all worthwhile ethical values. Therefore religion is a good starting point for an investigation into righteousness, or the source, nature and maintenance of ethics as this affects the individual and society. And this is the part purpose of the following chapters in investigating the foundations for an objective and unifying world religious understanding which transcends the frontiers of any particular church or world religion.

2 – Need for a unifying world religious consciousness

The urgent need for such a unifying world religious understanding, transcending the various great systems of religious belief in our fragile global village, cannot now be questioned. Its function would be to act as a medium for peace between peoples, and as a moral instrument for resolving the many problems in communities worldwide. The ecumenical movement of the Christian churches towards a unity of understanding is but a first tentative step in that direction. Far more is needed, far faster. The looming threat of conflict between the Islamic and Christian civilisations; the ever-present strife between Jew and Arab; and the need for creating a mutual understanding of values between the cryptic East and the industrialised West, are issues demanding the attention of us all.

The cause of universal but true religion far transcends the narrowing cultural restraints of the great world beliefs now jostling with one another for a pre-eminent position. A true religious sense does not begin through ideas imposed by a powerful organisation but through the strivings of the heart, and through feelings which are a mixture of conscience and a love of goodness for its own sake. A religious sense is a natural human attribute and may arise without the pressure of any organised body. In its pure and healthy state it does not crave for superstition or idols, or mysticism – or even for a deity, but rather for peace and harmony and the good in all things, and particularly for the goodness which may be found in human nature and the trust for which this craves.

But a religious sense is not even necessarily confined to the human species, as in the past, has always been assumed. We may believe it belongs in no small part to the horse or the dog. The love and loyalty of a dog for its master or mistress is something which transcends the merely rational, and cannot wholly be explained as the reciprocal response for food and shelter. In this context, Sir Edwin Landseer's moving painting, *The Shepherd's Chief Mourner,* portrays an animal expressing the pain of grief which is no less intense than that to be found in any human heart. The adoration of the animal for the human, despite all the failings of the latter, is so deeply felt in its appreciation of goodness as almost to express a consciousness of awe and mystery. When the dog barks in defending his master's territory, it is not so much out of anger as out of a sense of self-righteousness, and this may be perceived even in the animal's facial expression and body language in appealing for approval. The religious sense is intuitive rather than rational, and this is why it cannot be assumed as being exclusive to homo sapiens.

In the same way that a true religious sense is not necessarily initiated through organised religion, so likewise, an irreligious sense is not necessarily a reaction against organised religion. Again, an irreligious sense is a kind of natural albeit undesirable human attribute towards others and the world in general. The irreligious type has usually an irritable disposition, an underlying cynicism, and an unpleasantness with those with whom he is thrown into daily contact.

In common parlance, the person with a *natural* religious sense (not to be confused with the religious devotee who is attached to a church or sect) is usually seen and described as a *good* person, irrespective of his or her beliefs in any organised religious system. Indeed, church membership *per se* tells us little about the personality of an individual. This is because an organisation is comprised of many psychological types, and when we talk about a natural religious sense, we are describing a particular psychological type, but types as such cannot be fitted neatly into the organised categories of a society. Those with a *natural* religious sense are perceived not merely as good but as somehow *blessed*, for their goodness and integrity, and a general benevolence which is not entirely explicable. They are merely sensed by neighbours, acquaintances and others as morally better human beings than those around them.

Likewise, in common parlance, the person with an *irreligious* sense, is often perceived and described as a *bad* person because of his unpleasantness and seeming malice, but this says nothing about his formal or alleged beliefs in society. Indeed organised religion has not only been typified by bad persons at certain times and places in history, but by persons of unmitigated evil. This, then, would seem to present a contradiction, for many might choose to argue the point that Torquemada, Tetzel or Pope Alexander VI, were "irreligious" despite their formal commitment to the cause of religion, but as we have said, a clear distinction must be made between those who fall into organisational categories in society as contrasted with those who fall into defined psychological types.

3 – Ethics as an insoluble philosophical problem

Therefore, if we are to make any sense of the true purpose of religion as striving towards ethical goals which are objective and universal, we must concentrate on the idea of the natural religious sense, for only through that may we find those values universal and underpinning all great religions.

There are also two other reasons as to why religion is a good starting point for the discussion of ultimate ethical values. The first stems from the fact that there is no agreement amongst philosophers as to a definitive starting point for the investigation of ethics. On what hypothesis, if any, must ethics be based for a critical examination of its study: on Utilitarian values (our own English empiricists); on the sense of duty (Immanuel Kant); on intuitionism (Martineau and others); on the intended outcome of actions (the Jesuitical or other theories of means justifying ends); on Pragmatism (Dewey, James, Dr. Schiller); on the adoption of the idea of the original position (i.e. social contract theories, Hobbes, Rousseau, or Rawls); on ideas of determinism or evolution (Marx or Bergson); or on some other system of subjective or objective thought?

4- Practicality of the religious sense

Since the purpose of religion must be the achievement of the ultimate good, there is inevitably a practical value in turning to the religious sense, or inspired intuition, or conscience, as a possible first step in the attempt to fathom out an understanding of ethical values. It may be agreed unequivocally (even by non-believers) that the value of this purpose of religion is unique. The unique value of this special intuition, as something of immediate practical importance, is not replicated in other spheres of the religious mental experience.

There are two reasons for this: firstly, because of the identity of ethics with the purpose of religion; and secondly, in the realisation that although the starting point for this approach to ethics may entail a journey into the unknown, the outcome is not ultimately unknowable.   Religion in this context thus becomes an inspired vehicle for discovery, fulfilling the function of a guiding star for the achievement of intellectual truth.

5 – Ethics subordinate within the wider realms of religious righteousness

The second of these reasons as to why religion is a good starting point for the discussion of ultimate ethical values, is that its concern transcends the subject matter of ethics within a greater cosmic framework. Hence we may trace a source from which ethics may be said to evolve, i.e. the religious consciousness. As Sidgwick has pointed out, "the primary subject of ethical investigation is all that is included under the notion of what is ultimately good or desirable for man; all that is reasonably chosen or sought by him, not as a means to some ulterior end, but for itself.   The qualification 'for man' is important to distinguish the subject-matter of Ethics from that Absolute Good or Good of the Universe, which may be stated as the subject-matter of Theology – taking 'Theology' in a wide sense, as involving only the assumption of some ultimate end of

Good, to the realisation of which the whole process of the world, as empirically known to us, is somehow a means, but not necessarily connecting Personality with this end of Good."[37] The present investigation will lead us to integrate the values of ethics and religion. The particular relevance of this and its practicality for our age, with its threats that go beyond the mere destruction of humanity, will soon become apparent.

This integration of values between ethics and the higher evolution of true religion, is also reflected in A.N. Whitehead's distinction between the influences of Social consciousness and World-consciousness: "A social consciousness concerns people whom you know and love individually. Hence, rightness is mixed up with the notion of preservation. Conduct is right which will lead some god to protect you; and it is wrong if it stirs some irascible being to compass your destruction. Such religion is a branch of diplomacy. But a world-consciousness is more disengaged. It rises to the conception of an essential rightness of things. The individuals are indifferent, because unknown. The new, and almost profane concept of the goodness of God replaces the older emphasis on the will of God. In a communal religion you study the will of God in order that he may preserve you; in a purified religion, rationalised under the influence of the world-concept, you study his goodness in order to be like him. It is the difference between the enemy you conciliate and the companion whom you imitate."[38]

6 – The need for sincerity

But such a discussion of religion in its broadest meaning, and of ethical values, cannot be embarked upon without that deep sincerity committed to the truth. This entails a critical analysis of all those objections barring the way to the substantiation of truth. Sincerity demands a profoundly serious approach to the issue in question. As Whitehead has argued,

---

[37] Henry Sidgwick, *Outlines of The History of Ethics*, Macmillan, 6th ed., 1931, p. 2.
[38] A.N. Whitehead, *Religion in The Making*, Lowell Lectures 1926, Cambridge UP, 1927, pp. 29-30.

"the primary religious virtue is sincerity, a penetrating sincerity."[39] In the sphere of religious experience it is not simply a question of easy "conviction," or that conviction itself should necessarily be taken as the criteria for measuring the desirable degree of the religious sense, for the proper definition of Sincerity is to be found in freedom, "from pretence or deceit, the same in reality as in seeming or profession, not assumed or put on, genuine, honest, frank."[40]

7 – The dangers of conviction

Conviction in action is too often an unsubstantiated quality – dangerous in the fanatic – and counter-productive – and too often wrongly used by those within the churches as a value in measuring religiosity and nearness to God. It is dangerous on account of its subjectivity, both in regard to the individual in his striving towards the understanding and life of ultimate values, and even more so in regard to the collectivity of any religious community. It is well known that collective feeling reinforces prejudice and conformism; tends to repress the healthy free will of the individual; and sets up a barrier to enmity (concealed or overt) against those who do not "belong."

Conviction, taken as a value, is too often and unknowingly used as a cover for false consciousness, self-deceit, or to fulfil a subjective psychological need. True religion – and few religious leaders would dare to question the contention – must transcend the mere subjective psychological needs of the individual, as otherwise religion is reduced to fulfilling a psycho-analytical function and is bereft of all authority with regard to world or cosmic issues or as an objectively based belief in God.

---

[39] Ibid., p. 5.
[40] Concise Oxford Dictionary, 5th ed., p. 1189.

8 – Contemporary crisis of the churches

But by the same token, a religion incapable of engendering an absolute conviction in its followers is meaningless, since it is without ethical power, becoming riddled with hypocrisy and moral corruption. This is the worldwide problem of the churches today, and it is made evident in four ways: firstly, through the declining percentage of persons in most countries associating on any regular basis with their own church; secondly through the general disbelief in God, or recognition of religion or for its need; thirdly, through the unsatisfactory relationship of churchgoers to the nature of religion in its purest sense, i.e. their hypocrisy, moral false consciousness, or use of the church as an instrument for achieving or maintaining social status; and fourthly, through the failure of the churches to act as a sufficiently significant social force for the good of the world community.

The apparent failure of the churches worldwide, in all the above spheres, has never been more evident than it is today. It should be noted that the response of church leaders to the accusation of their failure is threefold: it may be taken as a question of re-organising for greater efficiency, usually through incorporating better man-management techniques; it may be a matter of marketing more effectively the religious message; or it may be an issue of tampering with religious doctrine so that belief comes more easily to followers. All three approaches have been often tried, and all three have unhappily failed to result in any real or long-lasting good effect.

9 – Their unfortunate response to this

There is, besides, something morally questionable in these three approaches. This is because they are superficial or cosmetic *vis-à-vis* the true purpose of religion. This fact is sensed even by the agnostic majority whose interest in religion may be minimal. The antics of populism of many churches, irrespective of whether it takes the form of re-writing texts or revising the order or style of services, seem at worst cynical and vulgar, and at best meaningless and absurd. This is because these things have been undertaken whilst the core issues of religion and belief remain unquestioned, untouched and sacrosanct under the lone authority of tradition. If religion in its truest meaning is to be regenerated, then it is the core issues of religion which must be addressed and possibly re-formulated.

There are other church leaders who whilst recognising the short-comings of their organisations or sects, and whilst declining to press for change, will merely retreat into the known security of their own church. These leaders will often regard themselves as the realists amongst their church brethren. They have an apology rather than a response to the problems of the church: viz., that it is only the tiny minority who are anyway the elect, and that one cannot hope for, and that it does not matter that the majority remain apathetic to religion, or to the question of God's existence. The apathy of the majority is anyway fore-ordained. But such a dismissive attitude, although supported by Biblical authority, is grossly unethical, since it gives rise to a moral elitism (and all the consequential ills and arrogance resulting from this) which in its anticipated final outcome cannot possibly be supported by rational argument.

10 – The crisis of belief

Furthermore, this form of apology remains a poor defence of the contemporary state of religion, when the problem is simply no more than a general lack of conviction in religious belief. The question may well be asked, to what extent must religious belief be allowed to decline before the validity of any specific church must itself be subjected to critical scrutiny? The fundamentalist may argue that such a question should never be asked, on the grounds that measuring the popular acceptance of religion is an irrelevant criterion in ascertaining its truth. But in the real world, the decline of religion may fall to such a low level of appeal that the day is reached when its validity has to be called into question. How can the fundamentalist hope to justify his religion if he acts within a social void? How can he uphold his doctrinal principles if there is no one to listen to his message?

11 – When is religion destroyed by disbelief?

Leaving aside the attitude of the fundamentalist, when does a church, because of its decline in terms of followers, cease any more to be a religion in any meaningful sense? Of course the institutions of a religion may be maintained by any number of artificial means, and all manner of fancies and fads, but such institutions soon become moribund and devoid of all true religious significance.

These are the problems facing the churches in the contemporary world, and such problems can only be resolved by confronting the core purpose and issues of religion. And it is these prime issues which the churches refuse or dare not discuss in any depth, since they feel it may bring about the entire structure of doctrinal belief tumbling down upon them.

CHAPTER 6
Doctrines and Their Social Influence

"Religions commit suicide when they find their inspirations in their dogmas."

A.N. Whitehead, *Religion In The Making*, CUP, 1927, p. 110.

1 – Definitions of religion

There is one problem only facing the churches in the contemporary world, and that is the crisis in belief, or the lack of conviction which alone makes any religion meaningful. How can this problem be resolved?

It is necessary to consider the nature of religion. What is religion? In the words of Whitehead, "there is no agreement as to the definition of religion in its most general sense, including true and false religion; nor is there any agreement as to the valid religious beliefs, nor even as to what we mean by the truth of religion."[41] Lexicography and sociology may be researched in vain. The definitions of religion are many and diverse. The closest dictionary definition is merely, "one of the prevalent systems of faith and worship,"[42] which is meaningless in the attempt to elucidate the true and intrinsic nature of religion.

R.H. Thouless, in his study of the psychology of religion described it as, "a felt practical relationship with what is believed in a super-human being or beings;"[43] Tylor, the anthropologist, wrote that "a belief in spiritual beings," was a minimum definition of religion; Max Müller that it consisted, "in the perception of the infinite under such manifestations as are able to influence the moral character to man;" Matthew Arnold that it was "morality tinged with emotion;" Salomon Reich that it was merely "a body of scruples which impede the free exercise of our faculties;" and Julian Huxley as, "a way of

---

[41] Whitehead, op. cit., p. 4.
[42] COD, op. cit., p. 1048.
[43] R.H. Thouless, *An Introduction To The Psychology of Religion*, Cambridge, 1923.

life which follows necessarily from a man's holding certain things in reverence, from which his feeling and believing them to be sacred."[44] The reason for the lack of any authoritative definition of religion stems from the fact of its diversity throughout the ages.

2 – Primitive religion (or magic)

The religion of our pagan ancestors of eighty generations ago, for example, would not now even be recognised as religion according to our contemporary expectations of what a religion should mean. It would rather be denominated as magic, black magic, or even as witchcraft. It was merely concerned, in the words of Sir James Frazer, with "a propitiation or conciliation of powers superior to man which are believed to direct and control the course of nature and of human life,"[45] and by "powers" are meant, "conscious or personal agents." Such a religion had no concern with ethics in the course of ordinary life. To the modern man or woman there is little in such a religion that commends it in upholding a system of morality of any intrinsic worth.

3 – Religion in the classical world

The religion of the classical world had already lost its authority as a system of serious belief well over 600 years before the official establishment of Christianity by Constantine the Great in AD 324. The mainstream religion of the Greeks and Romans had degenerated into a mere aesthetic experience long before the intellectual and cultural highpoint of either civilisation, and it only became a moral force when the occasional philosopher, such as Cicero or Marcus Aurelius, used it as a source of inspiration for developing their own ethical ideas.[46] The gods of the classical world had so

---

[44] Julian Huxley, *Religion Without Revelation,* Max Parrish, 1957 ed., pp. 9-10.

[45] Sir James Frazer, *The Golden Bough,* Macmillan, 3rd ed., 1911, Vol. I, p. 222.

[46] See Cicero's, *De Republica; Scipio's Dream; The Nature of The Gods,* and, *Offices* (Treatise On The Moral Duties of Mankind), also the *Meditations* of Marcus Aurelius.

degenerated in the eyes of their alleged worshippers that they
had become the butt of scurrilous invention and the objects of
ridicule of sceptical poets.[47]

4 – The rise of Christianity

The religion of the dark ages and the medieval world
strove valiantly towards the attainment of truth and the
development of the religious spirit, and was so successful in this
that it created what is termed the Christian civilisation.
Nonetheless, the extent of this influence was not, as with the
later Islamic and earlier Eastern religions, totalitarian in its
extent, for its power was limited by or balanced against the
jealously held rights of secular authority: of the Ghibellines
versus Guelphs; of King versus Pope; of prince versus bishop,
and of nobleman versus priest.

5 – As a force for social good

This bifurcation of authority within the community acted
as both a good and bad influence on the cause of true religion.
Its involvement in conflict alone was sufficient to enliven its
interest in the existence of social ills; and the necessity of
strengthening its own organisation in confronting secular power,
ensured that a great part of that organisation was utilised for a
good social purpose, such as the establishment and maintenance
of hospitals and charitable arrangements for the poor. The bad
influence of this bifurcation of authority resulted in the
compromising of religious principle; of surrendering to the will
of wealthy patrons; of turning a blind eye to the oppression of
the downtrodden; and finally, of falling for the luxury and

---

[47]   Note such scenes of parody in the play of Aristophanes, as Poseidon hiding from Zeus'
observation under an umbrella, Trygaeus' ride to Heaven on his dung beetle, and Dionysus'
bargaining with the corpse; or Lucretius' philosophical poetical work, *De rerum natura*, that
sets out to free mankind from religious fears by proving that the soul is material and is born
and dies with the body, and whilst acknowledging the existence of the gods, maintaining that
they can neither help nor harm mankind. None of this, however, should suggest that religion
during the classical period was entirely devoid of spirit. Religious enthusiasm was chiefly
expressed through the Mysteries centred around the various oracular places of worship.

corruption of the secular life itself, so that the religious spirit became drained to its last dregs.

6 – Integrity of the Church Triumphant

There was a time during this period when the church was Triumphant, i.e. when the religious spirit came nearest to achieving the ideal of promoting the absolute truth as it could then be understood within the intellectual constraints of the time. This was during the 12th and 13th centuries, and especially during that period when Thomas Aquinas, the greatest of Western theologians and Scholastic philosophers exerted his powerful influence throughout Christian Europe. During this period it may be said that there was a greater integrity within the body of the Christian church than at any time before or since – excepting perhaps only for that short period during the life of the Apostles and its immediate aftermath.

7 – Thomas Aquinas and the search for truth

Bearing in mind the ignorance and superstition of the Middle Ages and the limitations of Thomas Aquinas when compared with the greatest philosophers of both ancient or modern times, he nonetheless remains a giant amongst Western theologians on account of his rigorous intellectual search for the truth. His true greatness lies in the fact that he recognised that the "end of the universe is the good of the intellect, i.e. *truth.*" He argued that "the pursuit of wisdom in this sense is the most perfect, sublime, profitable, and delightful of pursuits."[48] Partly because of the integrity of his purpose, partly because of his discovery and use of Aristotelian modes of thought, and partly because of the high value he placed on the intellect, of all theologians he remains amongst those who may least be accused of deceit or self-deceit. In the eyes of the ordinary man or woman of our own era he certainly possessed those characteristics that would gain him most credence and respect as

---

[48] Bertrand Russell, *History of Western Philosophy*, Allen & Unwin, 1946, p. 476.

a theologian, even if today many of his arguments and assertions can no longer be upheld.

8 – As reflected in the understanding of humanity

The glory of the Christian church during those centuries in its genuine striving for the objective truth, and in its real attempt to work for the social good of humankind on earth, is unlikely ever again to be repeated by organised Christianity. The glorious era was only tarnished by occasional outbursts of persecution against heretical sects, perhaps most notably by the cruelties perpetrated against the Albigenses. The glory of the Roman Catholic church during this period stems from its psychological understanding and sympathy for the human personality, and the reflection of this in the rites and organisation of the church, e.g. the idealisation of motherhood and the qualities of the leading saints; purification through confession; and salvation through good works. All this was embraced within an organisation committed to the practical business of the world, not only through the shared power of the church in the direction of government, but through agriculture, care of the sick, production of beverages, etc., of the different monastic orders. The Christian church at its best worked uncompromisingly for the good of the majority, even though it may not have been entirely successful in its purpose.

9 – Reformation no reflection of religious progress in its true sense

The Reformation quickly put an end to these ideals, and with the emergence of some of the nastiest religious leaders ever to have held sway, there followed a conflict that was to transform the nature of Western Christianity – both Catholic and Protestant alike. The intellectual power of Luther, and the validity of his critique of the Roman Catholic church as he found it, cannot be questioned. He found the church rotten and corrupt, and within several years of his condemnation of the sale of indulgences, he proceeded to damn it in the language of the utmost hatred. But if his critique was sound, time has long since proven that his theology was far amiss in its appreciation of human nature. It needs more to castigate a wrong to create a right.

10 – Psychological consequences of salvation through faith

This has been demonstrated by many German thinkers and historians who have studied the social effects of his teachings in the homeland.[49] But what more could have been expected of a man, who in the words of Christopher Dawson belonged to the "Middle Ages rather than (to) the modern world? ... He was entirely alien in spirit from the culture of the Italian Renaissance, and even from that of the Northern humanists, like More and Erasmus, whom he describes as 'the vilest miscreant that ever disgraced the earth.' ... Luther's religious work of reformation and simplification amounted to a de-intellectualisation of the Catholic tradition. He eliminated the philosophical and Hellenic elements, and accentuated everything that was Semitic and non-intellectual. He took St. Paul without his Hellenism, and St. Augustine without his Platonism."[50]

Perhaps most notorious in this context were his fulminations against the power of reason, when he declared, "Reason is the greatest enemy that faith has; it never comes to the aid of spiritual things, but more frequently than not struggles against the divine Word, treating with contempt all that emanates from God." Or again, "Whoever wants to be a Christian should tear the eyes out of his reason;" or, "Reason should be destroyed in all Christians."[51] This barbaric thinking, or rather, the *repudiation* of thought itself, was to set the pattern for all the political-religious evils of the following centuries,

---

[49] See especially, Johannes Janssen's 16 volume *History of The German People At The End of The Middle Ages*, English trans. pub. by Kegan Paul, Trench Trübner, &, B. Herder, London & St. Louis, 1896-1910.
[50] Christopher Dawson, op. cit., pp. 180-181.
[51] Quoted in Richard Dawkins, op. cit., p. 190.

and even today is responsible for the obscenities of Christian fundamentalism, especially as found amongst the evangelical churches and multitude of sects in America.

"Salvation through faith," the core principle of Lutheranism, is a fine notion for morality, but in the world of psychological reality, it has given rise to ills that negate the good qualities it might otherwise have had. Salvation through faith puts emphasis on the idea that in the eyes of God, bad thoughts are hardly less evil than the acts themselves. The psychological outcome of this theology has proven catastrophic in the country in which it first developed. A mind incapable of thinking bad thoughts is anyway inconceivable – not merely psychologically, but on grounds of physiology. Bad thoughts may be stimulated by any sense perception: a nail in the shoe, an unpleasant odour, impatience, and a hundred thousand other incidents with which we may be confronted daily. Theology, of course, is not concerned with such petty physiological causes of bad thoughts, but the examples must be cited in illustrating the nature of the mind as a receptacle incapable of totally excluding, from time to time, the occurrence of malicious or wrong thinking.

What was the psychological outcome of salvation through faith? The unnatural pressures on the human mind were so great that they led to numerous perversions: e.g., to thought control; to a loss of free will and a morbid dependence on some other individual or group; to inflexible modes of thinking; but most of all, to a huge sense of resentment and aggression. These characteristics, pursued in the socio-political sphere, were to mar German history for the following 400 years, but especially in the immediate 100 years following the death of Luther, when his country was reduced to a desert of burnt rubble, and consequently, progress retarded for the following 250 years.

11 – Questionable character of the Reformers

Furthermore, by contemporary ethical standards, it would be difficult to argue that the leaders of the Reformation were "good men," in the sense of promoting the wellbeing of humankind on earth. Indeed, that was not their purpose. They were only concerned with the welfare of the "soul" and the preparation for the "next life," and if a comparison is made between both the theology and works of Catholicism and Protestantism in the 16th century, it will be found that the latter were more obsessed with the "other world" (excepting only for the church in Spain) than their too often maligned enemies in the other camp. Even the integrity of Luther to the common principles of decency and justice must be called into question. The language of his fulminations against the Jews (which was anyway a curious anomaly in view of his enthusiasm for the Old Testament teachings) is reminiscent of the ravings of Julius Streicher in the 20th century.

12 – The poodle of the princes

Luther remained a faithful poodle of his powerful paymasters. When the peasants, who had earlier fallen under his spell, in several parts of Germany, appealed for his support against the oppression of the princes, he knew on which side of the fence his political bread had been buttered. Having exhorted the peasants to "suffer" and not to actively repel injustice in his tract, *On The Civil Power* (published in 1523); two years later, he went to the extreme of urging the princes to initiate a war of extermination against the rising peasants in a publication of May 1525. Consequently, on the authority of the church for the New Age, thousands of peasants were butchered, and the common man was quickly disabused of any thought of the good intentions of the reformer whom they denounced as the accomplice of their oppressors. Hence, the Lutheran church, far from becoming an instrument for social reform, became the tool of the ruling classes almost from the time of its inception. This was further emphasised by its recognition of the separation of power between church and state. This, then, was the alleged advance of Christianity!

13 - The dictator of Heaven on earth

If Luther was the poodle of entrenched secular power, then Calvin was a dictator in his own right, establishing a Christian rule of almost totalitarian extent. His most disgraceful action was the murder of Michael Servetus, a truth-seeking Spanish theological scholar, and the leading thinker behind Unitarianism. The two men had entered into a disputatious correspondence culminating in an intricate deceit, whereby the Spaniard was enticed into visiting Geneva, whereupon he was promptly arrested, tried and burnt alive at the stake. History records that Calvin's leniency extended to a preference for merely beheading Servetus rather than burning him, but his more fanatical followers won the day.

It is difficult to imagine how a man capable of such wicked falsity in practical matters could possibly be expected to maintain integrity in the discussion of more abstruse questions. The dogged ruthlessness of the Protestant reformers over every article of doctrine is well illustrated by the fact that both Luther and Calvin would gladly have burnt one another had they been afforded the opportunity.

14 – Psychological consequences of predestination

Turning to the theology of Calvinism, it is more outrageous (to the modern mind) than even that of Luther. Its central tenet is based on the idea of Predestination, i.e. that salvation and damnation are pre-ordained before even the moment of birth, and that there is nothing that man can do to alter God's inevitable will. This ruthless determinism is marked by Calvin's belief that every drop of rain and every thought of man represents a particular expression of the divine will. The psychological   implications   resulting   from   belief   in predestination were so far-reaching that they broke through the barriers of religion itself to be sublimated in the hectic world of work. Intense activity alone could offer relief from the awful threat of eternal hellfire. Much has been written by leading sociologists on the Protestant ethic and the spirit of capitalism, most notably by Max Weber and R.H. Tawney.[52]

This picture of the emergence of Protestantism should not suggest that the Reformation (or indeed, the Counter-Reformation) was not without its worthy martyrs, who in their humility, sought out the truth without tarnishing the ethical integrity of their own personalities. But such martyrs, some of whom were prominent but the majority just ordinary men and women, were strong in the concentration of their faith but weak in the necessary cunning that goes with political acumen. Today their names are inscribed on memorial plaques in many cities of Europe, but their ashes have long since cooled in the intervening period.

To summarise, in the opinion of the great 19th century historian and statesman, Guizot, the Reformation had tended to retard than advance the cause of freedom in many of the territories it subjugated to its cause. In a famous course of lectures, he declared, "when the dominant party amongst the reformers were reproached with persecution, not only by their enemies, but by the children of the reformation; when the sects which they anathematised exclaimed, 'we only do what you did, we separate ourselves from you, as you separated yourselves from Rome;' they were still more embarrassed, and too frequently, their only reply was an increase of severity. ... two faults were committed – on the one hand, it neither knew, or respected all the rights of the human intellect; and while they claimed them for itself, it violated them elsewhere. On the other, it did not investigate how far the rights of authority, in intellectual matters ought to extend; - I do not mean that of coercive authority, which never can possess any right to interfere with reason; but of a purely moral authority, which acts

---

[52]   See Max Weber's, *The Protestant Ethic & The Spirit of Capitalism*, trans. by Talcott Parsons, Charles Scribner, NY,   1958; also, R.H. Tawney's, *Religion & The Rise of Capitalism*, John Murray, 1926.

only on the mind, and solely by means of influence. Something is wanting in the greater number of the reformed countries, to the good organisation of intellectual society; to the regular action of ancient and general opinions. The rights and the claims of tradition, have not been reconciled with those of liberty; and the cause of this must undoubtedly be sought in the fact, that the Reformation did not fully comprehend and accept, either its own principles, or effects."[53]

If these words had been spoken just over a hundred years later, i.e. after the Second World War, Guizot's remarks would never have been more apt or topical, as a reflection of the German church's failure to face an evil on a scale he could never have imagined. A prominent religious thinker and British historian late in the 19th century, has remarked on the Christian church that, "since the Reformation it has acted rather as a dividing than a uniting influence, and further, that through a great part of its history it has been a too consistent enemy of freedom. It has been over and over again the main support of tyranny; over and over again it has consecrated misgovernment, and retarded social progress; repeatedly it has suppressed the truth, and entered into conspiracy with error and imposture."[54]

15 – The atomisation of religion

And so what is the condition of contemporary Protestantism? With the exposure of the Bible to the subjective "inner light" of the individual, the Christian religion has been atomised into a thousand sects and factions, so that its intellectual authority has been shattered within the crucible of conflict. Now all the talk is of unity and cooperation, since any other path would spell the suicide of Christianity. And so the Lutheranism of today is a very different plant from that of its early years – hardly recognisable from that of its founding father.

---

[53] F.P.G. Guizot, *Lectures On European Civilization*, John Macrone, 1837, pp. 394-396.
[54] J.R. Seeley, *Ecce Homo*, Macmillan, Eversley ed., 1903, p. xix.

In the land of its origin it is keen to seize on every compromising and trendy modernism, and to turn its back completely on the embarrassment of an awkward past. So far has it gone in this striving, that shortly after the last War, it ditched its finest hymns of the 19th century – determined to repudiate the last vestiges of sentimentality characteristic of that era – in a gesture to transform its image. In repudiating its 19th century heritage, it thus threw away the baby with the bathwater. But its desperate attempts to update its marketing appeal have done little to improve its success, for everywhere congregations have withered as elsewhere throughout European Christendom.

16 – Its contemporary sterility

Materialism and apathy has everywhere seemed to rule! But thoughtful critics of the church – those sympathetic with the power of true religion – have argued that the German Evangelical church has become spiritually moribund. If this is true, has this been due to its inherent nature? Was such a fate made inevitable by its early theology? It might also be added that there is probably a higher divorce rate amongst Lutheran pastors in contemporary Germany, than amongst religious leaders from any other community in any part of the world. How, then, can such a church pretend to represent the interests of family life without betraying some shade of hypocrisy?

Meanwhile, the Lutheran churches elsewhere have taken on the characteristic influences of their host countries: whilst in America they are "uplifted" and optimistic; in Scandinavia they are overcast by the gloomy Puritanism of a teetotal culture.

CHAPTER 7
Looking East and West

"It has been said that a people gets the government which it deserves: it can with at least equal truth be asserted that a people worships the gods which it deserves."

Julian Huxley, *Religion Without Revelation*, Max Parrish,
1957 ed., p. 12.

1 – Perceiving the evolution of religion

This introductory survey has been necessary in illustrating the diversity of religion and the difficulty in ascertaining a concise and exact definition of its nature. Nevertheless, there can already be traced an evolutionary process towards a higher purpose and spirituality.

Whilst primitive religion amounted to the mere propitiation of avenging spirits; in the classical world there at least emerges the existence of actual gods. Whilst these deities exerted little moral influence, religion became most significant in fulfilling various traditional formalities in the political life of the state. Such a religion had limited spiritual appeal. With the emergence of Judaeo-Christianity in the Near East, infinitely superior religions where introduced into both West and Eastern Europe.

2 – Islamic core theology in advance of Christianity

But our short survey cannot stop at this juncture. Our consideration has to include a brief mention of the very different religions of the East before a full understanding may be grasped of religion in its broadest context. The core theology of Islam, which belongs to the same family group of religions as Christianity, is far in advance of that of Christianity. The reason for this may be found in the fact that it was the last of the three great Semitic or Abrahamic religions to emerge on the stage of world civilisation.

To the Islamic Arab, Christianity is not simply wrong but almost pagan in the superstition of its beliefs. In Islam there is but "One God who is God," and his nature transcends precise definition or understanding. The "heathenism" of Christianity is not merely reflected in the "Three Gods in One" or in the mystical gymnastics of the Trinity, but in the eating of the God's body and the drinking of his blood as celebrated in the Eucharist. As anthropologists have long since pointed out, this is a ritual no different from that of primitive tribes found in many parts of the world.

3 – Limitations of belief in a personal God

The Christian priest or pastor never ceases to boast the superiority of his religion on the grounds that he has a "personal" God, by which he really means a "human" God, but to the Arab, this is not simply a contradiction in terms but a blasphemy. The idea of a personal or human God is inconceivable! Why should he be cast in the image of man? Man's smallness makes him an insignificant speck in the universe. God's greatness and omnipotence puts him above all comprehending by man.

Jesus, in the eyes of the Arab, is amongst the greatest and most revered of prophets – The Son of Man – but to describe him as God is to commit sacrilege against the name of Jesus himself. The Islamic Arab never tires of hinting to his Christian friend that, "God has no partners! He works alone as the One God!" There is nothing to fault the soundness of this theology in its appeal to the intellect, and in the 18th century, both Gibbon and Voltaire, amongst other thinkers, betrayed a warm sympathy for Islam, in contrast to the deficiencies of Christianity.[55] As for the spiritual content of Islam, no one can stop to doubt its power over the soul of man throughout the centuries.

---

[55] See especially the 15th and 16th chapters of Edward Gibbon's, *History of The Decline & Fall of The Roman Empire*, on the rise and influence of Christianity, comparing these with chapters 50 to 52 on the rise and spread of Islam; also, Voltaire's short story, *Bababec*.

4 – Backwardness of Islamic social life

If, on the contrary, one turns to the practical life and the legal system (the *Shariah*) imposed by the Islamic religion, a very different picture emerges of its civilisation. Here we see a culture that in many ways is still locked into the dark ages, or more correctly, into the attitudes and thinking of the Old Testament. As we have noted above, the Islamic religion, through the *Koran*, and more especially the *Hadith*, exerts an almost totalitarian influence over the everyday life of its followers. The five daily calls to prayer – each day according to a different time schedule in accordance with dawn and dusk – are merely the basic requirements of the true believer. Numerous other detailed daily obligations are required, in regard to ablutions, diet, modes of eating, forms of expression in a variety of circumstances, and sexual practices, etc.

As for the *Shariah* law with its public floggings, amputation of limbs (legs as well as hands), beheadings and stonings, ceremoniously executed after Friday prayers, these seem an anachronism to the European when perpetrated in countries otherwise enjoying every convenience and luxury that the technology of Western civilisation has to offer. Such punishments are carried out more in the spirit of an all-avenging Jehovah of the Old Testament, than in the name of an "All Merciful God," whose title is reverently inscribed at the beginning of every legal document in the Islamic world. It is hard for the Westerner to appreciate the meaning of the Most Merciful God as he watches a public stoning, as described so horrifically, for example, in Geoff Carter's illuminating book, *Death In Riyadh*.

5 – A religion which prevents progress

But the critique of Islam goes far beyond the question of alleging a brutality or injustice against the dignity or rights of the individual. In this respect, the Westerner's perception may indeed be tinged with his own subjectivity, for the problem of crime and punishment goes far beyond the mere shock reaction of the visitor from another culture. A discussion of much greater length is required on the question of society's retribution on the wrongdoer.

The real problem of Islam and the case for reform, is that it acts as a barrier to technological development in a similar way that the Medieval church blocked material progress prior to the Renaissance. This is a supreme irony for it was during the medieval period that the Islamic world was far in advance of Europe in science, medicine, mathematics and philosophy – most of which Europe gained (or regained) through Arab sources. The difference between the two historical situations, however, is that whilst the medieval church actively sought to block material progress through the persecution of outstanding innovators and discoverers; contemporary Islamic civilisation is faced by a cultural barrier which only unconsciously prevents the successful implementation of a technological society.

6 – The three reasons for this

The causes of this cultural barrier may be brought under three headings: firstly, the practical problem of the total division of labour between the sexes, whereby a man and woman are forbidden to come face to face[56] (at least in the more orthodox Islamic states); secondly, a reluctance to engage seriously in any kind of work which deviates from buying or selling; and thirdly, a restrictive psychological block stemming from sexual repression arising from the intensive puritanical nature of the Islamic religion. This third factor is perhaps the most significant of all, since it limits the ability for relaxed thinking and adaptability, so necessary in learning and implementing the practices of a complex technological society.

---

[56] This comes under the law of Illegal Seclusion, whereby a criminal offence is committed if an unrelated man or woman are left together in a room or lodging. Strangely, the law is not deemed to be contravened if a European electrician or plumber visits an Arab household when only the women are present. However, the consciousness of illegal seclusion is so strongly felt, that I have met Arabs who would refuse to enter a lift in a London hotel if a woman was also present.

The technological clumsiness and backwardness of the Arab peoples is due to cultural factors and is manifested in many spheres of activity. Most recently it may have been seen in the Iraqi conduct of the first Gulf War, where despite immense wealth and the presence of the most technically advanced hardware, there was a poor use of strategic resources and an incompetent handling of weaponry. If the Arab peoples are to emerge on an equal footing with those of Europe and the North American continent, then substantial changes would have to be realised within the Islamic religion itself.

7 – The threat to Islamic civilisation

This is not to suggest that there has to be a Westernisation of thinking, or even of practice, for that could amount to a mortal blow to Islamic civilisation. If all the inhibitions and customs of Islamic life were to be dropped by edict to align with Western values, this would inevitably lead to the meltdown of the culture and unmitigated chaos. The worst of all possibilities would then be realised with a purely negative outcome. The result would be comparable to those clashes of culture and their consequent demise as seen amongst the indigenous peoples of North America, Australia, Africa and elsewhere. Hence a highly sensitive approach needs to be taken in considering this wide-ranging problem where a religion has dominated every aspect of a people's outlook. The required changes can only be initiated and achieved from within the body of the Islamic community under the leadership of their most intelligent and far-seeing thinkers.

8 – Contrast between the Islamic and Sino-Japanese civilisations

In further demonstrating that it is the *nature* of the religion that has acted as a brake on the advance of technological civilisation within the Islamic culture, we might usefully turn to the Far East in noting the very different religions of the Sino-

Japanese peoples and the contrasting results of their contacts with the West *vis-à-vis* the development of new technologies.

Before considering the religious cultures of China and Japan, there are two factors which may be noted: firstly, it needs to be borne in mind that not only are these cultures situated at the opposite side of the globe from Europe, but shortly after their discovery by the West, for some 200 years, both China and Japan closed their doors to all influences from the "foreign devils." Secondly, the Arabian Islamic civilisation of the Middle East and North Africa had always maintained its contiguous contact with the European powers, both politically and commercially – most significantly during the later period through Turkish suzerainty at the Sublime Porte. In view of these factors, what then happened in the modern era to cause these different cultures to react so differently to the introduction of Western science and technology?

9 – Religion responsible for these differences

The clue is only to be found in the dissimilar nature of Sino-Japanese religious thinking – for neither of these peoples, in adopting Western technology, have either sacrificed their own intrinsic cultures or the core values of their civilisation. The most dominant religion in influencing the thought patterns of the Sino-Japanese might indeed be denied the status of a religion in the eyes of the Judaeo-Christian peoples of the West, according to their narrower definition of what constitutes a religion. This is because the religion now in question is not only humanistic in spirit but is devoid of any metaphysical system explaining the cosmos; and although it gives recognition to prayer, with regard to the living, it has little concern about life after death. Furthermore, it has no sacred scripture, church, clergy or creed, no belief in heaven or hell, and so no instruments which may be used for persecution, bloodshed or conquest. But since the statues of its founder may be seen throughout temples in the Far East, alongside a medley of other deities, and since the philosophy of the faith is deeply ingrained in the habits and attitudes of the people in their daily life in social intercourse both in work and at home, as a sociological factor of existence, it cannot be denied the definition of a religion.

10 – The nature of Confucianism

This particular religion has an honourable standing which puts its foundation 500 years before the birth of Christianity. Its precepts are based on upholding the "five constant virtues" of humanity, righteousness, propriety, wisdom and faithfulness. It has always been cited as the religion of civilised values, and since it has always been concerned with the affairs of this world rather than the next, its teachings are steeped in the practicalities of achieving an ordered and harmonious society, where mutual love and respect may be experienced throughout society in all the many circumstances of human contact. Its central message is that good actions contribute towards a healthy state of mind as a first step in creating a balanced and integrated personality.

11 – Contrasted with the Abrahamic religions

Although its teachings are profoundly moral, there is no all-avenging God or the threat of hellfire, and so its followers, unlike those of the three great Abrahamic religions of the West, are not psychologically crippled by the concept of Sin. But the teachings of this religion go far beyond moral or social matters. They extend to philosophy, aesthetics and science, placing a high regard on the intellect and the virtues of study. It is also one of the very few religions strongly imbued with a long tradition of scepticism. The name of this religion is Confucianism.

12 – The value of religion is in its sociological outcome

The value of no religion should be judged from a dry-as-dust academic viewpoint. There is no intellectual activity more pointless than the weighing of differing theological doctrines. As Whitehead has pointed out, "what is generally disputed is doubtful, and what is doubtful is relatively unimportant – other things being equal."[57] A.G Whyte has argued, "of all forms of religious controversy, the most barren is that which directs itself to the criticism of particular dogmas. The sole result of such an attack is the discovery that the position assailed has been abandoned, virtually if not officially, as non-essential."[58] A religion should therefore only be judged according to the sociological effects exerted on its followers.

The overriding influence of Confucianism on the Sino-Japanese peoples is omnipotent in all spheres of life, despite the presence of other beliefs to which certain sections of these peoples might adhere. The prime force enabling Japan to become the mightiest industrial nation on earth has been the spirit of Confucianism. The same influence has been responsible for enabling the industrial success of the Chinese economies of Taiwan, Hong Kong and Singapore, as well as that of Korea, and latterly mainland China itself.

13 – Sanity of Confucianism contrasted with the dualism of the West

Several years ago two prominent British industrialists, both committed Christians, with a long experience in the Far East, confided to me on different occasions their dismay at the realisation of how Judaeo-Christian values had contributed to splitting Western society through the contradictions of dualism and the biting consciousness of Sin.[59] This dualism is manifested through God versus the Devil, Heaven versus Hell, or the Good versus the Bad. In Britain, especially, this dualism has been sociologically reflected in an orgy of class hatred and industrial conflict. My industrialist friends were quick to point out that the societies of the Far East are free from this dualism

---

[57] Whitehead, op. cit., p. 4.
[58] Adam Gowans Whyte, *The Religion of The Open Mind*, Watts & Co., 1913, p. 15.
[59] Sir Charles Villiers, who died two days after these thoughts were expressed was one of these industrialists, and Sir Peter Parker was the other.

and conflict, and that the cultural influences of Confucianism had so smoothed the path of personal relationships that such patterns of hatred were inconceivable.

The industrial conflict of the West, seen from across the globe, is perceived as absurd – as senseless self-destruction – as the suicidal nonsense of the psycho-pathologically sick. Scholars in the West have since written in some depth on the sanity of the Confucian society in comparison with the divisiveness engendered by the Judaeo-Christian tradition.[60] How has Confucianism so successfully achieved such harmony in society? It has been achieved by what has been described as "water logic" in contradistinction to "rock" or dialectical logic, i.e. the dualism of the conflict of opposites used as a tool in problem solving which has characterised Western mental processes since the time of the ancient Greeks.

Water logic, on the contrary, necessitates the saving of face in all those situations when differences of interest may occur between individuals or groups. Face saving not only entails a stipulated code of conduct but an attitude to life. It is the key to social harmony and industrial dynamism. Of course Western businessmen in a negotiating situation with the Sino-Japanese have often been exasperated and left in a quandary by this face-saving civility that turns a "No" into an unacceptable gesture. Agreements have to be reached by a process that defies the path of Western logic.

14 – A better approach to inventiveness

Several contemporary thinkers have gone further even in their appraisal of Confucianism than regarding it merely as a source for social harmony. Dr. Edward de Bono, of lateral thinking fame, for example, has detailed the mental processes of Confucian thinking of the Japanese in their greater inventiveness in the car industry, in contrast to the lower degree

---

[60] See especially the writings of the Japanophile, Prof. Ronald Dore, formerly director of the Institute for Intermediate Technology. His book, *Taking Japan Seriously: A Confucian Perspective On Leading Economic Issues*, Athlone, also, *British Factory Japanese Factory*, are well worth reading.

of innovativeness found in the same industry in America, on account of dialectical modes of thinking.[61] Whilst the innovative mental processes of the American – or other Western person – take the form of asking, Where can I find faults or deficiencies in this product to counter them with improvements,? The Japanese simply asks, How can I improve or build upon what I have already achieved? He has no need to waste energy on the dialectical process of searching for faults, and his direct or positive mental processes will anyway disallow him to think in this fashion.

15 – A developing religion

As with Christianity and Judaism, Confucianism is a developing religion. Indeed, if it was a rigid system, it would hardly have been capable of helping transform the Sino-Japanese cultures into such an industrially world leading position. It should also be noted here that there are substantial differences in the traditional background between the politico-economic and ideological systems of the Chinese and Japanese peoples. Nevertheless, the underlying influence of Confucianism in *both* cultures has suddenly come to the fore in enabling the utilisation of Western technology for the greater good of their peoples – at least, in the Far East states of Japan, Korea, Hong Kong, Taiwan and Singapore, which are unique amongst the nations of the world.

16 – The dynamism of Singapore

This returns us to the contrast made with Islam, which is not simply embarrassed by Western technology and materialism, but is increasingly averse to it. Although the Arab peoples are pleased to utilise the technological luxuries of the West, they accept this technology with a grudging fatalism and a minimum understanding at its face value, and if an appliance

---

[61] In a lecture delivered to the ACME Conference at the Olympia Exhibition Centre on 12th November 1991.

is difficult or falls into disrepair, it is simply pushed aside and forgotten. The existence of this technology has in no way affected their philosophy of life. Contrast this with the situation of the Sino-Japanese peoples. In this context I have had some experience of Singapore. It is only necessary to take up a copy of the *Straits Times*, and peruse through its pages, to discern that its people comprise an exceptionally vibrant society. Every day, many pages of this newspaper are packed with advertising material for educational courses of every conceivable kind: for German, Russian and Japanese; for business and computer systems; for deportment and charm; for English literature and mathematics; for art appreciation; for meditation, yoga, etc., etc. Once on the island, one quickly realises that here are a people who experience an intensity and joy in life. On the MRT (Massive Rapid Transport system) the local railway network, great numbers of young people are reading not the pulp literature too often found amongst youth in the West, but serious books on philosophy or science. This reflects the high value placed on study by the religion of Confucius. It should be noted, however, that many of these go-getting "Confucians" have lately become Christian converts – usually entailing membership of the free churches – but as good Chinese this does not diminish their underlying Confucian values.

17 – Women more liberated than in the West

Everywhere there is a curiosity and friendliness. Women have at the same time a modesty and frankness, and a tactile charm of innocence, hardly to be met with in the West, indicating clearly a freedom from the psychological complexities of original sin. Even if nominally she happens to be a Christian, her unspoilt soul remains set in the Confucian mould. Before Western feminists pontificate on the need for "liberating" Eastern women, they should better look into their own repressions, when all too often there will be found a failure to address true feelings to the objects of their affection until time is long past the possibility for a reciprocal response.

This is not to suggest that Eastern women are free of all disabilities, but with the current progress of industrial culture, there is every indication to believe that in several years any imbalance of inequality will be amply redressed. And neither should the above be taken to suggest that Singapore is a hedonistic society, for the serious intensity in creating an industrial infrastructure is linked into the same purpose of a healthy materialistic joy in life. Furthermore, Singapore presents a classless and harmonious multi-racial society – even though the preponderating majority of Chinese comprise 70% of the population.

The joy and dynamism of Singapore can only shame the West into a consciousness of the latter's spiritual decline – and what may be said of Singapore, may also be said of the other Far Eastern states. And with regard to Britain, a symptom of that decline of spirit may be demonstrated simply by a per capita comparison of productivity. A trip to the Far East, for any Briton, presents a sober lesson as to the future of this country! It is a remarkable irony that a 4,000 year old civilisation, seemingly stuck in a time warp for 300 of those years until the 20th century, should now seize hold of the torch of Western technology and science as jealously as if exclusively its own.

18 – Healthiness of the Confucian soul

And the credit for all this must be given to the religion of Confucius, which has created a healthier psychological soul, so enabling the practical progress of her peoples. Whilst the religion of Confucius is committed to the matters of this world, Christianity stands in a midway position, whilst Islam, with its restrictive – even punitive – puritanism, stands at the other end of the spectrum. The psychologically repressive influence of the latter is alone responsible for holding back the true inner liberation of the Islamic peoples, for only with the achievement of that liberation can they succeed in maximising the benefits of science and technology for their better use.

CHAPTER 8
Why There is no Best Religion

"An unhesitating appeal to reason as our only test of truth
seems to be not only an admissible method of study, but the
only method of study consistent with regard to truth, and the
only method which can issue in serious beliefs."

H.M. Gwatkin, *The Knowledge of God*, T. & T. Clark,
Edinburgh, 1931 ed., p. 3.

1 – Contemporary relevance of Buddhism

Before leaving this general survey of religion, there is one
other great system of belief we must touch upon, for a
certain leading aspect of its teaching has an extraordinary
relevance for our time. This is Buddhism.

Buddhism is a religion of great diversity which has
developed separate strands in different parts of the world. It
grew out of Hinduism, as a deeply spiritual sect, repudiating the
pantheon of that religion, at about the same time as the rise of
Confucianism. There is no space here to elaborate on its
complex doctrines, or the cycle of life in the world of
transmigrating existence, but the prime significance of
Buddhism in all its manifestations, lies in its description of
man's relationship to the universe and his environment. This
puts it in sharp contrast to the Judaeo-Christian tradition.

2 – Contrasted with the Abrahamic religions

Judaism and Christianity have always put man at the
centre of the universe, and as the greatest of all creatures, as the
master of his earthly environment through the strength and will
of God. The earth and all it has to offer – its forests, land,
minerals, animals and fish of the sea – are there for the
exploitation of His Glory, i.e. both God's and man's. Man
through God alone is the Master of all!

This super-confidence giving an ethical rationale for the rape of the environment, puts man on a far higher plane than the pagan religions of primitive times. At least our pagan ancestors, as well as primitive peoples in their religious thinking and practices worldwide, deferred to the greater glory of the earth. The tree spirits were appeased before the timber was cut. The fertility goddess was propitiated as the precious seed was broadcast, and as invocations were made to the rain god, respectful recognition was given to the powers of nature.

3 – Our pagan ancestors respected the environment

With the rise of monotheism, however, the power of God in nature increasingly became an abstraction, until there evolved an all-jealous God who became the sole focus of worship, and the nature and the environment lost the hold of its respect on man, becoming only an object for ruthless exploitation.

The early missionaries from Ireland or Rome mocked our pagan ancestors, for their reverent gestures to the powers of nature, as meaningless superstition. The cowled celibate in his dirty sackcloth glanced disdainfully at the joyful Saxon youth as he surveyed the rising sun in the forest glade. The new religion had no room and no time for the glorification of nature. God in Heaven alone was to be the object of man's worship, for this world was merely a trial for the next, and only the hereafter had real meaning. The new religion was to have immense significance in changing man's relationship with his environment.

4 – Buddhism is a religion for the environment

But Buddhism had none of the characteristics of the paganism of the past. It arose as an ethical movement against the superstitions of Hinduism, and it has developed a greater respect for our earthly environment than any other religion before or since. This respect is not embodied in a mere sentimentality or inexplicable awe of nature, but in something far more profound and practical as a way of life, viz., a developed ethical system. The reverence for life has become so great that even the accidental destruction of the smallest insect is regarded as a wrongdoing.

To the Buddhist, man is not to be seen as the master of nature but rather as an integral part of it, and this status gives him no right to a special place or controlling superiority to do as he chooses. In this context Buddhism may be seen as the religion for our time in carrying through the ideals of environmentalism, and in the need to maintain a balanced ecology. Although in the West it is still very much an esoteric religion, it is attracting ever greater numbers of people who realise that Christianity has nothing to say on these urgent contemporary issues. Of course there are people who will desperately scratch around for Biblical texts to counter such a contention, but it remains an inescapable fact of tradition that Judaism and Christianity have created theologies that are extraordinarily difficult to identify with the interests of the environment.

5 – Its kindness to the animal kingdom

One aspect of this different relationship – and increasingly there is a changing attitude in the West, as reflected through the growth of vegetarianism, protests against cruel sports, etc. – is in regard to animals. More than 100 years ago, Schopenhauer, who was a friend of Buddhism, pointed out the "fundamental error of Christianity, an error which cannot be explained away, and the mischievous consequences of which are obvious every day: I mean the unnatural distinction Christianity makes between man and the animal world to which he really belongs. It sets up man as all-important, and looks upon animals as merely things.

"Brahmanism and Buddhism, on the other hand, true to the facts, recognise in a positive way that man is related generally to the whole of nature; and in their systems man is always represented, by the theory of metempsychosis and otherwise, as clearly connected with the animal world. ... Christianity contains, in fact, a great and essential imperfection in limiting its precepts to man, and in refusing rights to the entire animal world. As religion fails to protect animals against the rough, unfeeling and often more than bestial multitude, the duty falls to the police; and as the police are unequal to the task, societies for the protection of animals are now formed all over Europe and America. In the whole of uncircumcised Asia, such a procedure would be the most superfluous thing in the world, because animals are there sufficiently protected by religion, which makes them the objects of charity."[62]

Even the small child in the West realises the illogical stupidity of Christianity when he buries a treasured pet and is told by a parent, in the name of "truth," that as it has "no soul," it will not find a place in Heaven. This reflects the absurd self-centredness of Judaeo-Christian, and indeed also, of Islamic doctrines.

6 – Eastern view of Western religion

What must be the view of the peoples adhering to the great uncircumcised religions of the East to the religious systems holding sway in the Western world? Firstly, there must be incredulity and pity at witnessing religious conflict. Surely there must be a contradiction in terms! How can the peoples of the West be said to lead the religious life, or a life according to the moral principles of true religion, if they kill and terrorise one another over petty tenets of doctrinal belief? – for this is how these troubles are perceived half a world away. Surely this is not religion as it should be!

When the man or woman from the Far East reads the history of Western religion, he reads nothing less than a history of horrors. How different this is from the history and nature of religion in the East. In the East, if religion means anything – is anything – it is peace, harmony, understanding with the cosmos and humanity, and the pursuit of the eternal verities and the good

---

[62] Arthur Schopenhauer, *Essays*, Allen & Unwin, 1951, Sect. III, "The Christian System," pp. 73-74.

life. In the West, to the Eastern mind, it is hardly any of these things, for instead, it is interminable squabbling in the pursuit of unity; differences over form and ritual whilst substantial issues are pushed aside; even a battle between the sexes for priestly privilege; and a sordid controversy over the sexual orientation of those who may lead the congregations of their church. All this seems hardly to be religion! And most of all: should not the value of a religion be measured by the devotion of its adherent in both belief and practice? Now look to religion and contrast the East and West!

7 – No one religion superior to the rest

To the student of comparative religion in the West, it is increasingly apparent that there is no one system of religious belief which can justifiably claim superiority over the rest. This is sensed by the ordinary populations of Europe and it is manifested in several ways. Apart from the awareness of the general decline in religious feeling in the West, and the increasing appreciation of the value of local religions as part of the intrinsic cultures of their peoples, it is perhaps most manifested through a growing disgust at the idea even of sending missionaries abroad to "civilise" the natives. Whilst it is still applauded that men and women should be sent abroad by their religious orders to fulfil specific practical functions in medicine, food aid, agricultural or anti-illiteracy projects, etc., it is becoming increasingly unacceptable that they should be sent to proselytise. The idea of the evangelising missionary, armed with a Bible, spreading the "word," is today becoming an object for contempt.

8 – Insensitivity of missionary activity

There are several reasons for this, all concerned with the insensitivity of the proselytising process. Apart from the fact that the missionary is seen on all sides as the harbinger of the materialistic "goodies" of the Western world, with all their price tags, his "message" too often proves the death knell of native cultures. To what extent can the missionary, with all the arrogance of his "superior" faith, hope to understand the mental processes and moral standards of his hearers? What understanding does he have of the local religion, and what understanding of its moral worth as an essential contribution to its intrinsic culture? The missionary would first have to be an anthropologist before he becomes a proselytiser if he or she were to show a proper sensitivity in addressing native peoples.

And if he cannot understand the mind of the native, and more important, the different nature of his spirituality, how can he hope to ascertain the inner response to his religious teaching? And when the culture is half destroyed by this Westernising influence, and the physical and mental ailments of the West are inflicted to a tenfold degree on these peoples of a distant land, is not this a discredit to both the Christian religion and the people on whom it has been so forcefully imposed?

9 – The "White man's" religion

There are today parts of the world, e.g. in Africa, and amongst sections of the black population in America, where Christianity is seen as nothing more than the White man's religion, and where Jesus is perceived as the White man's tribal god. Outrageous as this may be, it remains a real perception. Who then must bear the onus for the existence of such attitudes, irrespective of whether the latter may be substantiated from an objective viewpoint: the preachers or missionaries who first spread the "word," or the mistaken holders of such opinions? No simple answer can be given, for in the final analysis, it is the sociology of religion and the socio-political interaction of peoples within a broad cultural framework that marks its stamp on the character of a religion.

10 – Conserving primitive cultures

How different is the attitude of the contemporary European to the evangelising missionary compared with that of only fifty years ago! He was then seen as a heroic battler, bearing the torch of truth and civilisation against the darkness of ignorance and superstition. Today, the cultures of Third world peoples are no longer regarded as either ignorant or superstitious, but as deserving respect in their own right, irrespective of how they may diverge from our own subjective standards. Our contemporary view is that the many primitive cultures in the Third world are delicate flowers, precious to the heritage of the world, and that their needs are primarily material linked to a sensitive appreciation of their very different spiritual and cultural requirements.

It is not Christian missionaries who need to be sent to these distant lands, but Anthropological missionaries who may effect necessary change whilst at the same time endeavouring to preserve the essence of the native cultures and their specific values.

In summary, on this topic, we may conclude with the remarks of Christopher Dawson, when he wrote that, "the modern criticism of the great religions is not altogether devoid of foundation. Their intellectual absolutism and their concentration on metaphysical conceptions have tended to turn men's minds away from the material world, and from practical social activity. But this preoccupation with the Eternal and the Absolute and the spirit of 'otherworldliness' which it generates is antipathetic to the modern mind, since it seems ultimately to destroy the value and significance of relative knowledge – that is to say of rational science – and of human life itself. The present age seems to demand a religion which will be an incentive to action and a justification of the material and social progress which has been the peculiar achievement of the last two centuries."[63]

---

[63] Dawson, op. cit., 238-239.

CHAPTER 9
The Decadence of Contemporary Religion

"It is the Christian, not the so-called Atheist, who has been pleading for a 'non-miraculous Christianity.' The men who have written articles and books to prove the impossibility of believing in the Virgin Birth and the Resurrection of Christ (as once interpreted) are men in Holy Orders."

Adam Gowans Whyte, *The Religion of The Open Mind*,
Watts & Co., 1913, p. 17.

1 – Religion's decline wrongly attributed to sin

Having made a survey of religions within the broad context of time and space, it is now easier to attempt a meaningful definition of religion for the new age. But before embarking on such a definition, what good purpose is there in making the attempt?

The purpose is that man is by nature religious, having a deeper inner need for religion. But that fact should not be used as a rationale for stuffing any particular religion down his throat. Religion is not something to be imposed, and indeed, in the modern world, it cannot be. If religion does not come to the individual of its own accord, then it remains of little value.

Today the churches have only a partial appreciation of this. When churchmen and churchwomen look around and see a spiritual desert caused by the spread of materialism and hedonistic values, they take on the guise of the Old Testament prophets, blaming this on the people for the loss of religious belief and on the ever-present existence of Sin. It is the wrong-heartedness of man that has brought this loss of faith! And because of ancient doctrines, and even current theology, it is difficult for churchmen to see this decline of religion in any other light.

2 – Conventional religion has lost its credibility

But Sin is *not* responsible. The churches can no longer blame the ordinary man or woman for this loss of faith. The church has simply lost its credibility as an exponent of truth in the eyes of the majority. It is the church which must take the blame for religions' decline, not the people. It is the church which has betrayed the people with its sickly propaganda, its insulting of the intelligence, its cheap emotionalism, its unsubstantiated dogmas, and its feeble intellectualism. It is not the people who have betrayed the church. These assertions are partly supported by the fact that the Good and Bad can in no way be divided according to churchgoing or non-churchgoing habits or religious belief.

3 – The agnostic often a better person than the churchgoer

The pews of our churches are filled with hypocrites, financial swindlers, promiscuous lechers of every sexual orientation, and wrongdoers of all sorts. And yet at the same time these are the complacent unthinking self-selected minority destined for "eternal paradise" – or so they think. In truth, they are not even religious in any proper sense. The least sinning amongst them, in the words of Whitehead, are merely "good people of narrow sympathies ... apt to be unfeeling and unprogressive, enjoying their egotistical goodness. ... They have reached a state of stable goodness, so far as their own interior life is concerned. This type of moral correctitude is, on a larger view, so like evil that the distinction is trivial."[64] What kind of morality can be expected of a church when its better adherents are of such a hue? The more ethically sensitive will simply refrain from churchgoing in disgust.

As a churchgoer over many years, I have met many non-believers who through their benevolence, consideration, humanity, and goodness in all their relationships, are more deserving of eternal reward than the cliques who are so primly self-assured of their superiority above the rest. Whilst the first

---

[64] Whitehead, op. cit., p. 85.

are often decent, tolerant, good-humoured and adaptable to the needs of commonsense; the latter are too often pinch-lipped, rigid, quarrelsome, arrogant, and above all, dependent on a restrictive source of authority, often defying reason and the better nature of humanity.

The non-believer is often a better person than his opposite since he believes in and lives by a higher code of ethics. The believer is too often bound by the constraints of subjectivity, is incapable of analytical thought, and is too quick in the misuse of platitude for every occasion. If the churchgoer is obsessed with a sense of his own sin, and is constantly at prayer and filled with contrition, there is either a sound reason for his guilt and miserable countenance, or else he is suffering from a pathological condition. Freud dealt successfully with many such cases. The virtuous unbeliever, on the contrary, often has a relaxed and happy nature, and his good deeds are spontaneous and unthought-of acts, not consciously carried out to please the dictates of a fearful heavenly master.

4 – Failure of the churchgoer to extend his intellectual horizons

But the worst characteristic of the "loyal" churchgoer is unquestionably the narrowness of his intellectual horizon, from which most individual and social ills are allowed to flourish. The failure to acquire freely available knowledge, and to use that knowledge to think through substantive issues facing himself and the community, is the abuse of God's greatest gift to man – the brain! The churchgoer tends not merely to pride himself on the narrowness of his vision, but to actually place ignorance on a pedestal. He justifies this attitude by asserting that the Bible alone is the source of all knowledge and wisdom.

More than a century and a half ago, Karl Marx wrote about religion as the "opium of the people." If his remark had a contemporary meaning and was aimed at the Continentals, then it was misplaced, as 19th century Europe was the battlefield of constructive revolutions; but if, on the contrary, it was aimed at the British – his adopted homeland – it was a well-placed remark. Elie Halévy, the great French historian of 19th century England, demonstrated in his magnum opus that it was the influence of religion alone which saved England from the revolutions of that era. A saving influence indeed! What was the truth behind this "opium" of religion?

5 – Methodism and the retardation of social progress

It was fortuitous for the establishment that John Wesley had spread effectively his Methodism throughout the developing industrial areas of Britain shortly before the industrial revolution. In doing so, he not merely successfully inoculated the working class against any possibility of participating in revolutionary activity, but actually turned the British working class into the most docile and stupid proletariat of anywhere in Europe. How was this achieved? It was through utilising the cleverest psychological methods[65] and Hellfire preaching, whereby men and women in their thousands were first aroused into uncontrollable enthusiasm, before being reduced into a state of whimpering subjection as converts of a religion which killed off the last possibility for political free thought.

If Wesley had been in the pay of the most unscrupulous band of capitalists, he could not have succeeded better in creating a class of willing slaves to feed the mills and mines of early industrial Britain. At the time, his methods were satirised by Hogarth on the grounds of "Credulity, Superstition and Fanaticism," and attacked by reputable church leaders for their revolt against the laws of reason and propriety. In the words of William Sargant, "the Methodist revival ... helped condition the English of the early nineteenth century to accept social conditions which would have caused revolutions in most other European countries. Wesley had taught the masses to be less concerned

---

[65] John Wesley was a precursor of the Communist authorities in Russia and China in experimenting with brain-washing techniques. A Leyden jar, for the electrical shock treatment of prospective converts may be seen to this day in the John Wesley Musuem, City road, London. This treatment was used on those whom he had already reduced to a state of hysteria.

with their miserable life on earth, as victims of the Industrial Revolution, than with the life to come; they could now put up with almost anything."[66]

Although Methodism has long since turned "respectable" and repudiated the proselytising methods of its founders, it should be borne in mind that the movement was in all probability the most significant influence in blocking social progress in early 19th century Britain. Had Methodism never existed, it is tempting to imagine how the establishment might have been overthrown under the benign inspiration of such men as Paine, Godwin, Place, Blake, etc., before establishing a legal system and government based on Bentham's, *Principles of Morals and Legislation*. Unfortunately, that was not to be, and up until the present time, the different churches in Britain have continued to oppose intellectual enlightenment of any kind on the grounds that it might give rise to the type of "freethinking" which is seen as such anathema (and perhaps wrongly) to Christian doctrines. Consequently, the churches have continued to applaud ignorance, regarding intellectual speculation as an evil only conquerable through the blind enthusiasm of faith in an intervening God and a blessed afterlife.

6 – Religious thought has lagged behind secular thought

But today such a critique of Christianity's negative social influence is almost an irrelevance, for the majority have so lost their interest in the meaning of conventional religion that they are not even prepared to listen to the issues let alone to participate in a dialogue. And the reason for this, as we stated at the start of these chapters, is the crisis in belief which is the underlying problem of contemporary religion. But this should not be interpreted to mean that the majority are inherently non-religious. Talk to any man or woman in depth and it is soon possible to find that he has his own god. It may not be a true god, but it nonetheless reflects his potential receptivity to a true faith.

---

[66]   William Sargant, *Battle For The Mind*, A physiology of conversion and brain-washing, Heinemann, 1957, pp. 219-220.

The reason for the crisis in belief is that theology has lagged far behind the intellectual development of Western thought in other spheres of activity. This, of course, is no recent occurrence. The evolution of theology along lines of credibility, has lagged in its development since the time of the Renaissance, for the consequences of the Reformation were an irrelevance in this regard. The quarrels between Catholics and Protestants, and the division of the latter into an infinite number of warring sects, only amounted to a regurgitating of already discredited doctrines – i.e. discredited from the viewpoint of credulity in the eyes of post-Medieval man. In the outcome of the Reformation, therefore, the evolution of theology should not be seen as having achieved a higher level of truth. All that was achieved was a correction of existing abuses, and the establishment of a multifarious variation of age-old doctrines, all in conflict, and none that could claim a preponderance of the truth by any objective standard.

7 – How religious doctrines were imposed by law

What was the result of this? Firstly, the different churches maintained their authority through secular power. Belief was simply imposed by law, and unquestioned by the passive majority. The Thirty-Nine Articles of the Anglican church, for example, needed to be subscribed to by university entrants almost up until the middle of the 19th century. This meant that both Catholics and Non-Conformists – not to mention Jews – were denied the right to a higher education. During the wars of religion the doubters of one religion or another were simply burnt or put to the sword.

This mutual persecution by the churches is no indication that truth was destroying falsehood, but that falsehood was merely fighting with falsehood. If the representatives of *real* truth were pushing forward their cause, what need would there have been for the vicious acrimony, and the tearing and burning of limbs to prove a doctrinal point? It rather indicates an inner doubt and conflict, an irritating frustration that could only be resolved by violence but never by argument. And all those disputatious issues have not been definitively resolved to this day. And does it matter? Apparently not to the wider world with its more deep-seated and urgent problems, and little even to churchmen and churchwomen themselves in an age with its emphasis on ecumenicalism.

How can all these conflicting doctrinal issues, then, be described as truths, when at the time of their hot dispute they were decided by the sword and today they are merely laid aside? Surely truths, in the sense of eternal verities, have an urgency which always lives. If a cause is worth dying for, surely it should be over a concern of demonstrable facts. But truths of an intellectual or mental kind are usually of such a self-evident nature that they arouse only moderate feelings one way or the other. Such are mathematical or scientific truths, or the truths of the spirit conveyed in great works of art. Most theological tenets, unhappily, do not fall into any of those categories. They are of a very different kind.

8 – And passively accepted until the present day

The consequence of the religious persecutions of the past on the majority was merely ennui and alienation. That is the reason why the peoples of Western Europe are less concerned with organised religion than almost all other peoples throughout the world. Conventional religion is no longer either a matter for protest or acceptance. Today the majority of the population of Europe (especially in the North) nominally accept their religious status without dissent or the wish to "doubt," even though inwardly they may be non-believers and socially-imposed hypocrites. Only in those countries where a church tax is levied do significant numbers of people declare their agnosticism so they may evade the levy. No self-fulfilling person wants to quarrel with the church in the 21st century any more than he did in the 16th. To keep your head low is always the wisest course! Such is the distance of the majority from their own religion.

9 – Religion is now too often only an aesthetic experience

Secondly, the decline of religious belief has been replaced by religion as a purely aesthetic experience, where doctrine and belief is taken not as based in truth or worthy of serious intellectual consideration *per se*, but purely as something comforting and convenient in satisfying different life situations. Perhaps this most of all is what has debased the coin of contemporary religious value. Amongst churchgoers, this aestheticism is most often experienced through the expression of song – the ostentatious voice out-singing the rest is to be found in most congregations; or in listening to the fine prose rendering of the King James version – when the intonation is what matters, not the meaning; or in contemplating the rhythmic movements of an elaborate ritual with all its colour and sound.

The non-churchgoer, on the other hand, benefits from the celebratory aesthetic experience of the Christening of his child; the married couple would be loathed to forego the ceremony of a church wedding; and the dying cherish the pretence of entry into a better world, whilst their relatives value the tasteful pomp of the funeral dirge and the slow procession to the last resting place as a fitting gesture of respect for a beloved friend or relative.

And as for Christmas, no one of good cheer would choose to forego this annual festival, even though its Christian message is lost on the majority. It is a festival that in the 21st century has reverted to its pagan origins in the Roman *Lupercalia* and that of other festivals of peoples in the North. But it may well be asked, does this festival differ overmuch in its meaning to the majority today, in terms of joy and goodwill, by comparison with the similar aesthetic experiences of our pagan ancestors in celebrating the Winter solstice? Were our pagan ancestors in welcoming the re-emergence of the sun any less benevolent in their feelings and sense of generosity towards their loved ones and the tribe, and did they enjoy their groaning board with mead and roasted hog any less than our contemporaries with their Christmas turkey and Claret?

It may be noted that the comparable atheistic endorsed weddings and funerals in the old Soviet Union (several of which I have attended) were perhaps no less meaningful to their subjects, and hardly less impressive in their ceremonial and words of wisdom, than the religiously endorsed weddings in the West. In both East and West, the meaning of these ceremonies extended little further than the aesthetic experience.

10 – This compared with that in the classical world

In sociological terms, the aesthetic experience of the contemporary church differs little from the experience of religion during the greater part of the classical period. In both there is a vague sense of awe at witnessing the formal ritual in an attitude of respect, but little more that is meaningful; and in both, after the congregations of temple and church have dispersed, there is expressed a gentle scepticism of belief and laughter at the priest who lost his footing or the tenor of his lines.

This aesthetic experience of religion, however, has been most significant in its influence through the expression of the arts: in both the classical world and Christian civilisation, producing the greatest monuments in plastic form and painting ever created by humankind.

11 – Medieval theology suited medieval man

The intellectual lag of theology in the post-Renaissance world in its failure to maintain credibility with the majority, can best be illustrated by contrasting the Medieval with the modern mind. The theology of the Middle Ages was ideally suited to the Middle Ages, but modern theology, despite all its intellectual efforts, is quite unsuited to the task. Medieval man was able to *believe* because in the light of his mental development, and within the constraints of his reasoning powers, there was little to suggest to him that he should *doubt*. If he was told that the world was created in 4,004 BC, on what evidence should be disbelieve the fact? If he was told the story of Elijah ascending into heaven in a chariot in a whirlwind of fire, of Balaam and his talking donkey and the angel with the drawn sword blocking his path, or the parting of the Red Sea so that the Israelites might escape to their homeland, there was no reason why Medieval man should doubt their literal truth in a world still haunted by spirits and hobgoblins and fiends in every conceivable shape and form, and when miracles still made their appearance by the dozen.

Even the great reformer, Martin Luther, was subject to these hallucinatory fantasies, and it is said that the ink stains can still be seen on the walls of his cell in the Wartburg, where he had hurled the writing materials at an assortment of menacing fiends which were interrupting the works of his diatribes against Rome or his translation of the Greek New Testament. Medieval man not only lived in a fantasy world of magic and irrationality, but he thrived on it through his romantic legends and literature. The Bible, if and when it became available for the knowledge of the ordinary man or woman, was in every way a book for the Medieval period. In no passage did it overstretch his or her sense of credulity.

12 – Modern Biblical teaching unconvincing

The same cannot be said today. Of course theology has re-adapted its approach in a brave attempt to maintain the appeal of the sacred texts. Literal interpretations have necessarily been repudiated in favour of the metaphorical, but figurative meaning in a text can only be stretched so far. If the entire contents of a book take on a metaphorical meaning, meaning itself is destroyed. This becomes inevitable through the ambiguity and conflict of interpretation. Where is any meaning left? It may be a bounteous gift to the sermoniser, who every time he sets his eye on the same text perceives a different message. His face may light up in a smile of inspiration, as he seizes pen and paper, in having seen yet another gem in the well-worn words, but this is hardly a reliable mode for uncovering the inner truths of religion.

It relies too heavily on subjectivity, and makes Holy writ every man's own opinion but not necessarily his neighbour's. The Holy book is cheapened by this metaphorical approach, for the meaning of language is denigrated as it takes on an oracular function in the hands of every religious amateur with a "personal message."

CHAPTER 10
How Ethics Relies on Truth

"Why does knowledge free us? Because, as we know more, we recognise that what we desire, hate, love, take pleasure or find pain in, has been the result of chance and accidental association and conditioning. To know this is to break the association."

Alasdair McIntyre, *A Short History of Ethics*, Routledge & Kegan Paul, 1967, p. 144.

1 – Ethical retardation of modern religion

This brings us to the argument at the crux of these chapters – to considering the most baneful influence of this lag of Western theology in meeting the needs of intellectual progress. This entails the ethical retardation of religion resulting from its failure to meet the demands of truth.

2 – The meaning of truth

The attainment of truth is the first rule for the realisation of righteousness, and truth must be the first precept for true religion. No church leader would question these statements, but the perception of truth changes as one era follows another. This is not to suggest that truth is subjective or relative, for those are pernicious notions contributing to lazy thinking, cynicism, or the pursuit of ulterior ends. Even worse is the idea of truth according to the philosophical pragmatists. Truth is only advanced by knowledge and is invariably entrenched in the firm ground of objectivity. There is no space here to discuss the conflicting notions on which it is based, e.g. the Correspondence or Coherence theories, or Tarski's Semantic Conception; but any discussion of righteousness, irrespective of whether or not the latter is conceived as a theological doctrine, must be based on fact.[67] More specifically, a statement must be seen as true if it corresponds to a fact and false if it fails to do so. As A.G.Whyte has so neatly put it, "believers must give reasons for the faith that is in them; and these reasons must be given in the legal tender of thought, realisable on demand in the authentic coin of fact."[68]

How lacking in integrity, in matters of faith, are today's clerics? The question needs to be asked, for it is secretly asked in the hearts of millions of laymen again and again. The rock foundations of the faith of the Medieval cleric could be trusted as true, but the same cannot be said of their contemporary descendants. There are too many tell-tale signs indicating that today's churchmen are compromising and unconvinced. To what extent are they influenced by the dictates of the vested interests of their particular church? As Whyte has noted in his penetrating book, "no one is more helpless in this world than a penniless clergyman who has left the church."[69] It is my suspicion that clergymen are no less dogged in pursuing their vested interests, even when it destroys the credibility of their religion; than are manufacturers in their dogged support of rentier capitalistic practices, even when it destroys the profitability of their productive enterprises on which they depend for their livelihood.

3 – Applying truth to religion

In the general discussion of theological or Biblical issues, commonsense should be used as a general guide in ascertaining the truth of any fact. Every theological assertion should be approached with the highest intellectual integrity through appreciation of the relevant spheres of knowledge. A knowledge of philosophy, or the latest critical techniques of symbolic logic, is not sufficient in approaching all the questions of religion.

There must be a true understanding of the nature of the *Spirit*, and that means a profound appreciation of psychology, for

---

[67]   For a more detailed discussion on the nature of truth, the following books should especially be consulted: G.E. Moore's, *Some Main Problems of Philosophy*, Allen & Unwin, 1953; F.H. Bradley's, *The Principles of Logic*, Macmillan, 2nd ed., 1922; and, Rudolf Carrap's, *The Logical Syntax of Language*, 1937.

[68]   A.G. Whyte, op. cit., p. 26.

[69]   Ibid., p. 5.

without this, religion is nothing. When a priest or a Protestant pastor comforts or otherwise assists a distraught parishioner, it should not be as someone over-keen to impart a single-minded message, but as a psycho-analytical healer, and for this purpose he must be sufficiently well-read and practised in the appropriate discipline. Only in this way will truth be fully realised. This is because religious truths are only found in human understanding, and human understanding is only found in psychology.

4 – Fighting superstition and falsehood

For the greater part of its history the church has pursued its intention of fighting against superstition and falsehood. This has been an excellent principle, even if not entirely realised in fact. The church must continue to fight against superstition and falsehood, but in the light of a higher sphere of knowledge. No grounds must be given for over-stretching the credulity of the ordinary person, for that is counter-productive to the cause of true religious faith. If churches are once again to be filled, and the majority drawn to the precepts of religion on the grounds of faith as opposed to aesthetics, then sound reasons must be presented for the acceptance of that faith. Unsubstantiated assertions or baseless hypotheses must be laid aside, and the so-called truths of revelation should be subjected to very critical review.

5 – Church leaders must maintain intellectual integrity

Above all, theologians must look into their own hearts as to their intellectual integrity. On reading through their tracts one cannot but doubt their own sincerity. A book that immediately comes to mind is Charles Gore's, *The Philosophy of The Good Life.*[70] Gore was a Bishop of Oxford and a leading theologian during the first half of the last century; a prolific writer and a man of considerable learning. He presents a critical albeit sympathetic study of ethically-based world religions in ancient and modern

---

[70] Charles Gore, *The Philosophy of The Good Life*, Gifford Lectures 1929-30, John Murray, 1930, later re-issued in the Everyman series.

times, and his integrity is intellectually irreproachable until he puts his mind to Judaism and Christianity, when his integrity falls apart, and an otherwise perfect book is spoilt by bias and mental gymnastics. It is unfortunate for the faithful of our own religion that such subjectivity should always be allowed to break through.

Why should the credulity of the ordinary man or woman be stretched: For what rational purpose? Nothing, except the decline of institutional religion! Of course there has to be faith. Religion without faith would not be religion, but there is nothing achieved for either the benefit of humankind or the cause of cosmic truth, if he is presented with religious doctrines which he finds untenable. In that situation, the churches act not as messengers for the truth, but involuntarily as vehicles for the spread of agnosticism and atheism. They then undermine all eternal verities they may once have promoted. The task ahead is to lay the foundations for a new religious consciousness for the new millennium.

6 – Bible abused as a work of revelation

Here is not the place to repeat all the criticism of religion or the Bible, or to associate the Christian rites and festivals with their pagan origins. All that has long since been discussed by Conyers Middleton and Voltaire and ten thousand others up until the present time.[71] But it is relevant to question the use of the Bible as a source for the revelation of truth, and there is undoubtedly some justification for the traditional Roman Catholic attitude in giving a lower priority to the popular readership of the Bible in favour of intervening texts to prevent the occurrence of confused or false ideas. The divisiveness of the Bible in a "free for all" environment, has already been touched upon, and there is not only an absurdity but a blasphemy in the subjective abuse to which it is constantly exposed.

---

[71]   Readers may wish to consult Conyers Middleton's, *Letter From Rome, Showing An Exact Conformity Between Popery & Paganism* (1729), and his tract *Free Enquiry* (1748). Voltaire's Biblical criticism may predominantly be found in the volumes of his *Dictionaire philosophique*. A far more scholarly work, however, based on extensive anthropological research, is Sir James Frazer's *Folklore in The Old Testament*, Macmillan, 1918, 3 vols.

It is too often a tool for the lazy or narrow minds of laymen who will not or cannot, or have not the time, to extend their intellectual horizons into the sphere of ethics but who nonetheless are driven by an inexplicable urge to pontificate to their fellow beings. If they exert an authority, it is as humble personalities, and not as the representatives of any proper or organised body of knowledge.

Worse than this, however, is the arrogance of the Bible thumping layman, whose reading and knowledge of the things of the mind often extends no further than this single book. As a teacher of the truth, he is often a social liability, who at any time may inflict harm rather than good – and the seriousness of this contention will be substantiated in the next chapter.

7 – Bible not an ideal source for ethical teaching

The suitability of the Bible, for contemporary use, as an ethical work transcending all others must be called into question on several counts, for its metaphorical interpretation, however far that may be stretched, still cannot belie its gaping deficiencies for modern use. Let me record a subjective response to this most famous of all books.

As a small child I was horrified by its violence, its acts of injustice purporting to be wisdom, and frequently, its downright stupidity – e.g. King Solomon's method of ascertaining maternity, or the selection procedures used in raising an army. Powerful leaders, for example, who struck dead bearers of bad tidings, seemed to my childish mind, not merely to indulge in senseless but in inconceivable acts of barbarity. What crime had the humble messenger committed? These were stories about primitive nomads who had not yet reached the first rung of civilisation, and as such, their psychology was incomprehensible and meaningless to modern man. Not even the wickedest tyrants of the 20th century killed the messengers who brought them news of defeat. My impression of these blood-curdling tales has not changed in 60 years, and as with the vast majority of people, I feel an instinctive aversion for the book when regarded as a source for true morality.

8 – An example of this

A few years ago I saw a 4-year old child perusing through a lavishly illustrated children's bible. Not far into the book was a two-page spread depicting the flood, including drowning animals and people, and babes in arms, all in a highly distressed condition. Fascinated, the child asked its mother, "Why are the people drowning?" – "Because they're wicked," answered the mother. – "Did they all drown,?" asked the child. "Yes, all," said the mother. "Is the baby wicked too,?" asked the child. The mother was unable to answer this simple logic, but merely attempted to distract the child by turning to another page. It may well be asked, What impression of religion will this child hold in its heart on reaching adulthood; and more significantly, What opinion will it hold of a God capable of such atrocities?[72]

9 – Crimes of the Jewish God

This brings to mind the accusations of the great American thinker, H.L. Mencken, against the Jewish God, when he writes, "one finds him engaging in all sorts of bloody brutalities, some of them so revolting that even his own agents, recording them as in duty bound, are moved to something not far from moral indignation. ... Open the Old Testament at random, and you will quickly find examples of Yahweh's generally bad character. In II Kings ii, 24, he sends two she-bears to assault and devour forty-two little children because they have poked some childish fun at the bald head of his prophet, Elisha. In Numbers xxxi he condemns 32,000 innocent Midianite virgins to violation at the hands of his victorious Jewish army, and earmarks thirty-two for the special use of his high-priest, Eleazar. In Deuteronomy VII,

---

[72] This atrocious book is, *The Bible For Children*, retold by Bridget Hadaway & Jean Atcheson, with a Foreword commending the book by the Rt. Rev. Michael Ramsey, Archbishop of Canterbury. Published by Octopus Books in 1973, 8th impression 1979. The offending illustration may be found on pages 16-17.

1-2, he instructs the Jews to massacre the Hittites, the Girgashites, the Amorites, and Canannites, and Perizzites, the Hivites and the Jebusites, and forbids them 'to show mercy unto them.'

"In II Samuel xxiv he first inspires David to take a census of the Jews, and then proposes to punish it as if it were a crime, and with the utmost fury. With ghoulish cruelty he gives David a choice of penalties: 'Shall seven years of famine come unto thee in thy land? or wilt thou flee three months before thine enemies, while they pursue thee? or that there be three days' pestilence in the land? David chooses pestilence as the probable least of those afflictions, and is appalled a week later when his agents report that 70,000 Jews have succumbed – more than 5%, according to his census returns, of the whole population of Palestine. His horror, indeed, is so vast that he is moved to remonstrate, saying, 'Lo, I have sinned, and I have done wickedly: but these sheep, what have they done?' The answer is not recorded, but the inspired chronicler adds that Yahweh 'repented him of the evil.'"[73]

Another American author, Joseph Wheless, has written that the Jewish God, "reeks with the blood of murders unnumbered, and is personally a murderer and assassin, by stealth and treachery; a pitiless monster of bloody vengeance; a relentless persecutor of guilty and innocent alike; the most rageful and terrifying bully and terrorist; a synonym for partiality and injustice; a vain braggart; a false promiser; an arrant and shameless liar."[74] The Bible has been a book of extraordinary influence throughout the entire period of Christian civilisation, and in view of the above, is it any wonder that the latter, and especially religious history in the West, has been marked by a cruelty and ferocity of violence unknown elsewhere? Whitehead has aptly remarked on the Old Testament that, "this worship of glory arising from power is not only dangerous: it arises from a barbaric conception of God."[75]

---

[73] H.L. Mencken, *Treatise On Right & Wrong*, Kegan Paul, Trench Trubner, 1934, pp. 163-164.

[74] Ibid., p. 165, Joseph Wheless, *Is It God's Word?*, A.Knopf, NY, 1926, 2 Vols.

[75] Whitehead, op. cit., p. 44.

10 – Bible's influence in promoting strife and cruelty

Is it any wonder that Luther, Calvin, and innumerable other religious leaders were particularly unpleasant personalities when they modelled themselves on such a God – for it is the Old Testament that has always held the greater balance of influence amongst Reformers and dissenters? In the words of Whitehead, "the Gospel of love was turned into a Gospel of fear. The Christian world was composed of terrified populations."[76] Even today, wherever there is chronic civil strife, the influence of religion is not far behind the scenes, and in the 21st century the tendency is increasing rather than diminishing.

Not only may we witness the conflict between Protestants and Catholics on our own doorstep in Ulster, but more recently, the bloody war between Catholic Croats and Orthodox Serbs, whilst the rest of Eastern Europe remains a powder keg for similar strife – not to mention the on-going "War" between Jews and Arabs in the Middle East. It is a sobering thought on how very different our Western history might have been if our religious life had been inspired by such harmonious men as Confucius with their this-wordly wisdom; or by such nature-respecting men as Gautama Buddha with their will-renouncing spirituality.

11 – The Fall, as interpreted through the centuries

The most far-reaching philosophical charge against the Bible (since it is something that has influenced Christian thinking until the present day) stems from the allegorical story of the plucking of the apple from the Tree of Knowledge of good and evil. Now Eve was certainly guilty of an act of larceny and Adam was hardly less guilty as a reluctant accomplice, and because of this, both may have deserved their fate in being driven from the Garden of Eden, but that is not the point of the story. The central point lies in their alleged wrongdoing in the search after knowledge, for they could not develop as meaningful human

---

[76] Ibid., p. 63.

beings without the experience of good and evil, and neither could they even begin to understand the nature of ethical values. Until the moment they had eaten the apple, they had merely existed as mindless children in a purposeless void, with little more meaning than a barnacle fixed to a ship's bottom.

But the allegory has been interpreted over the centuries to mean that all knowledge is evil, and that a spirit of enquiry in any form is a defiance of God's Will. It is the command of a jealous God, fearful of losing his authority to another deity. It has been used consistently as an argument for oppression against those who would advance the cause of progress through open enquiry. Today the allegory is merely understood as an argument for denigrating the intellect in disputatious situations in contradistinction to emphasis on faith. The ignorant are the blessed, and the cursed are the searchers after knowledge!

This philosophy is not only outrageous but immoral. It is comparable with the punishment imposed by Zeus on Prometheus for passing on the secret of fire to man. The punishment of both gods was motivated through jealously, and so in this respect, neither is better than the other. No religion for our time should be allowed to decry the intellect.

All good understanding and all benefits for humanity stem from the goodwill of the intellect in its striving for the better life. How much more far-seeing were the later Greeks in incorporating the idea of the intellect into their systems of ethical thinking. Indeed their approach resulted in the indissoluble blending of ethics and theology as seen in Platonism.

CHAPTER 11
The Problem of Sexual Morality

"All confesties of faith are travesties of the idea of Jesus."

Ernest Renan, *Life of Jesus*, Everyman ed., p. 237.

1 – The sexual allegory

Something more must be said about the allegory at the start of the Bible, and its influence on our consciousness until the present day. This concerns the appearance of Original Sin and the eternal shame of nakedness.

The power of this sexual allegory is unique to the cultures of the world, and the repressive puritanism to which it has given rise in all three great Semitic religions has much to answer for in causing untold psychological damage to entire populations over the centuries. Enough has already been said about the effects of this puritanism on Islam. Turning to Christianity, all its most prominent teachers (barring the founder Himself) and especially Saints Paul, Ambrose and Augustine, were not simply obsessed by sexual issues but convinced that the act was sinful under any circumstances. Celibacy alone was the ideal state for salvation. The act was tolerated as a "sorrow" for those who had been blessed by a Christian marriage – and indeed it was essential for the propagation of the species – but if it became a pleasure, or was resorted to without the intention of fulfilling its biological purpose, a heinous sin had been committed.

2 – The power of sexual repression

It is extraordinary that for two millennia, over a great part of the world, humankind has allowed itself to be bent by the will of power hungry priests, and then cowed into maintaining submission to such unnatural doctrines. Guilt was instilled with the terror of eternal Hellfire by the tyrannical literate over the ignorant credulity of the easily led. Even today the same methods are used but in a milder form. As a small child I was brought up to believe that God's main pre-occupation during the hours of darkness was to look under the bedclothes of little boys to see if they were playing with their private parts, and that every act of sin was entered into a large ledger with its columns divided into debits and credits, in preparation for the day of reckoning.

Many years ago my wife had a close friend who was one of seven children of a Lutheran pastor.   She was a girl of irreproachable character: conventional, virtuous and pious, and held in high esteem in my wife's village. Old women in black would point her out to their granddaughters as a worthy object for emulation.   In the same village dwelt a loutish buffoon: noisy, rude, vandalising, frequently drunk on schnapps and beer, and despised by everyone except his boon companions. Twenty years on the pastor's daughter was confined to an asylum after the breakdown of a marriage of several weeks; whilst meanwhile, the village "lout" had not only reformed his character but become a successful businessman and was a pillar of society. My wife, who had a high regard for the ascetic virtues, wept on contemplating the contrasting fate of these two individuals, and at the idea that good character should be so ill-rewarded, whilst the village "lout" had made a success of his life.

Where was the justice of the world? None, according to Christian teaching!   The moral of the story is that whilst my wife's friend had submitted herself entirely to the teachings of the Cross, and been broken in the process; the village "lout" had simply revolted against the false morality of his stifling environment, through unconscious yet fortuitous circumstances, and in doing so, had decided his happy future. By revolting against conventional morality the "lout" had preserved his humanity; by submitting to religious dictates, my wife's friend had lost hers. Where is good and evil to be found in such a story? It confuses and defies the convictions of the proselytising Christian.

3 – How the church has destroyed spontaneity between the sexes

The Christian religion alone has to stand responsible for destroying spontaneity between the sexes; the chances for success and happiness of millions of married people; and of destroying even love itself. Christian theology, through its tradition and inescapable logic, has brought misery, suffering, and mental derangement to untold millions through its revolt against the nature of the human psyche. The realisation of these facts is only possible through the acquirement of knowledge, and the contrast with happier peoples from other cultures who are unaffected by the concept of Sin. As Kate Millett, has so nicely expressed it: "Medieval opinion was firm in its conviction that love was sinful if sexual, and sex sinful if loving."[77]

4 – Definition of sin

What is Sin? It is defined most simply as, "transgression against divine law or principles of morality."[78] But this is meaningless in terms of sociological reality. Divine law is a fine sounding phrase – or at least it is threatening – but what does it mean? Sociologically it is nothing more than the imposition of a code of conduct which is so ancient that its origins are lost in the mists of time. And because there is no evidence of its man-made nature, it is asserted and conveniently reinforced as having been ordained by God. But today, with all our anthropological knowledge, we know that this is but one out of a multitude of moral codes imposed by man on himself.

The question is therefore relevant: Why should sin be sin? Its real significance lies in its repressive power on the psyche. Sin is experienced as a deeply felt emotion: a conflicting mixture of fear, attraction, jealousy and loathing. Every healthy person wants to sin whilst repressing the desire. This is what distinguishes it from simple wrongdoing, such as greed, lying, or

---

[77] Kate Millett, *Sexual Politics*, Virago, 1989 ed., p. 51.
[78] C.O.D., op. cit., p. 1189.

selfishness, etc., which are without such feelings of psychological complexity. Even St. Augustine, in his *Confessions*, prayed for the existence of a celibate life whilst also adding the qualification, "but not now!" The psychological complexity of sin is sufficient reason to question its validity as a guide to morals. Of course there will always be inhibitions imposed by the force of deeply felt tradition, but there are points in a people's history when tradition must be questioned and changes sought in the cause of achieving higher truths.

5 – Sense of sin a poor guide to a fulfilled life

Bertrand Russell has observed that, "the sense of sin, and the fear of falling into sin, produce, where they are strong, an introspective and self-centred frame of mind, which interferes with spontaneous affection and breadth of outlook, and is apt to generate a timorous and somewhat disagreeable kind of humility. It is not by such a state of mind that the best lives are inspired."[79]

Sin is not unique, of course, to peoples who have been influenced by the Abrahamic religions. Anthropologists have uncovered puritan societies amongst primitive peoples in many parts of the world. The general conclusion of anthropological research clearly indicates that puritanical or repressed peoples are not simply less happy and well-balanced than their more relaxed neighbours, but that that they are invariably more vindictive to one another. Furthermore, it has been found that sexual violence, rape, and prostitution are far more prevalent in puritanical than in more relaxed societies.[80] This is a clear indication that puritanical influences (irrespective of their source) are not simply harmful to

---

[79] Bertrand Russell, *Human Society In Ethics & Politics*, Allen & Unwin, 1954, pp. 40-41.
[80] See especially the work of Margaret Mead in regard to this, particularly her book, *Male & Female*, Gollancz, 1949, where interesting studies are made between the puritanical Manus of the Admiralty Islands and the Cannibal Mundugumor of the Yuat River, compared with the happier and more relaxed Samoans and Balinese.

humanity but actually evil.[81]   No further proof is needed in demonstrating this fact.

There is no question that self-denying puritanism makes for unhappiness, and later in life, contributes to a mounting resentment. The old man, and the old maid, who have never enjoyed the physical pleasures of existence often feel they have "missed out on life" and been defrauded all along of its real meaning. The awful realisation dawns too late that they have been unfulfilled, and all because they accepted on trust the dire warnings and false values of parents and teachers. Many years ago I knew an elderly Orthodox Jew, a street sweeper in Lincoln's Inn Fields, who was eaten up with hatred against the entire human race because he had been taught to deny himself all the pleasures of life. His friends – or rather his acquaintances for he had few friends in any real sense – regarded him with pity, blaming his parents and environment for his pitiable condition.

None of this should be taken as an apology for a eudemonistic theory of ethics, for by the same token, fulfilment and happiness is not achieved by an opposite style of life, i.e. of lust and debauchery. It may be remembered that the last years of Giovanni Casanova were depressed and miserable, during that time when he worked as the librarian of the Count von Waldstein in the Chateau of Dux, where he finally died. A fulfilled life has to be meaningful, and the happy person on his death bed not only relishes the purposefulness of his life, but its sweet physical pleasures, some of them, possibly of an illicit nature. He is able to reflect that none could have enjoyed a more pleasurable life, and since it was also purposeful and without malice, he may die with a feeling of fulfilment and benevolence towards the world he leaves behind.

6 – Responsibility of the Christian preacher

The heavy responsibility that lies on the shoulders of the Christian preacher, and particularly the lay preacher – whose

---

[81]   In this context a dissertation could be made on the puritanism of the Islamic religion as being the primary psychological motivation for outrageous acts of terrorism and self-immolation – although account must also be taken of political causes as well.

puritanism often outweighs that of his more professional co-worker – in his work in the community, can now be seen. Bible knowledge is not a sufficient qualification for taking on such a task. On several occasions I have sat silent as young men (still wet behind the ears) have fulminated against the "heresy" of psychiatry to their congregations, arguing that "Jesus" alone is sufficient in healing the mentally disturbed. These ignorant fanatics, too strong in faith but feeble in knowledge, with little experience of *real* life, should be banned from the pulpit. They are entrusted with too great a social responsibility. The extent of their damage may never be known, but it is anyway so great that lives, happiness and sanity are threatened if not destroyed. This is why the intellect is important as well as the acquirement of real knowledge based on scientific criteria. Every preacher is concerned with spiritual values and the souls of his congregation, but the terms "spiritual" and "soul" must be understood in a demonstrable meaning, and not merely as the abstractions of some theological doctrine.

It may be that the churches use faulty criteria in selecting their preachers. It is anyway evident that many congregations have a significant proportion of young and older men who are not only single but appear uninterested in the opposite sex, or else, belong to that class of men who are permanently on the verge of an engagement which never actually materialises. These are the activists in the church who are so often keen on enforcing a puritanical code of morals on their co-religionists. Might it not be asked if a significant number of these men are repressed homosexuals who find in the church a convenient haven for sublimating their ideas of right and wrong, as well as a God for whom they feel a sexual as well as a spiritual love, which conveniently for this moral sense, may never be consummated as a physical experience? After all, the natural kill-joy has to rationalise his unnatural inhibitions, and what better theatre is there for such a purpose than the church with all its moral taboos? Shortly after our marriage, my wife remarked that surely a clergyman is the ideal husband, for such a man would never give another woman a second glance. A quarter of a century later she held quite the contrary view, for observation had told her that clergymen's wives were so often amongst the most miserable on earth, since in their husbands' eyes they always played second fiddle to God. And the necessity for a false front by these wives only worsened the pain.

I should not like the above descriptions and imputations to be interpreted as my general view of the clergy. For the most part I have generally found the clergy to be men and women of integrity, approachable, friendly, and intent on doing good for their parishioners, the community and the world at large. If this was not so, I would not now be raising the issue of church leaders and their congregations as foremost prospective supporters for a regenerated deism. Church leaders today *are* concerned with the physical welfare of peoples everywhere irrespective of their faith, and most significantly, they have a more disinterested attitude to political issues than could be hoped for from most party politicians. It is for this reason they are such a valuable asset in addressing the major problems of our time.

7 – Pathological sexual guilt special to the Abrahamic religions

All religions and cultures are concerned with sexual relationships in maintaining norms – indeed the complexity of such norms is often greater amongst primitive peoples than modern man[82] - but amongst the great civilisations of the world, the deep-seated guilt over the idea of the sexual act, or the thought of sex, is unique to the Semitic religions.[83] Because of the tenacity on thought of cultural mores, it is extraordinarily difficult for the people of any culture to develop an objective self-understanding of their condition. It is inevitable that the uninformed will always regard their own way of life as not

---

[82]   One of the most comprehensive studies on this aspect of primitive sexuality is Sir James Frazer's, *Totemism & Exogamy*, Macmillan, 1910, 4 Vols.

[83]   As observed earlier, this is not to suggest that Christian and Islamic societies everywhere are marked by repressive sexuality. The Islamic peoples of the Maldive islands (including the womenfolk), for example, are accounted highly promiscuous.

merely the best but the only conceivably acceptable mode of existence. I can cite an example of such a situation.

In the Middle East I was once given an ornate hubble-bubble by business friends, and some months later I returned with a photo of a friend and I using the gift in my home. In the picture, on a coffee table, were three cups, and a sharp-eyed Arab friend enquired as to whom the third cup belonged. When I explained that the cup belonged to my wife, and that two married couples had been socialising together, he was deeply shocked, immediately expressing his surprise to friends who were sitting around. Although he appreciated the wide differences between his own culture and that of the West, he still could not credit the idea that a "respectable" man would tolerate this social mixing of the sexes.

8 – Morality distinguished from Ethics

Exactly the same situation pertains in the reverse, i.e. honest Christians from the West will visit distant places imagining that "nice" people will always think and act as they do, although differing in a multitude of other "unimportant" ways. Whenever they discover that this is not so, they will seek to effect changes to their own standards of behaviour and thought, without the slightest realisation that this is a nonsensical approach. For example, Christians have a fixed idea on what they regard as the proper and only mode of performing sexual intercourse, and when they were confronted, to their horror, by a variety of other methods in colonial territories, they tried to enforce what has since become known as the "missionary position." Such cultural insensitivity only arises through ignorance, but it raises the entire question of moral standards to their realistic level. But this book is not about morals but about ethics.

Morals, from the Latin *moralis*, meaning custom, is only concerned with endorsing accepted standards of good behaviour and thought, but the idea of morality in Cheltenham may differ widely from that accepted in Jeddah, Saigon, Brasilia, Delhi, Accra, Beijing or Johannesburg. Moral standards only have meaning within their own cultural context, and cannot be transferred from one social environment to another without the risk of violating the latter. Such projected transfers in their defiance of commonsense rather resemble the attempt to put a dog's head onto a cat's body. They are both impossible and fatal operations.

Ethics, on the other hand, from the Greek *ethikos*, is concerned with questions of right and wrong in their broadest context, and not simply as judged within the criteria of accepted custom. The study of ethics entails a far deeper and more complex discipline than the mere study of morality. It is an ironic fact that the Christian church, supposedly concerned with ultimate values, has always given far more of its energy to the consideration of moral questions than to the more important and fundamental ethical values within which morality is contained.

9 – Narrow interpretation of Christian morality

In the light of the above observations, it is now possible to return more authoritatively to a consideration of the church's attitude to sex. The church's all-consuming obsession with sexual issues has even reduced the meaning of morality, in the common parlance of the ordinary person, to no more than sexual judgements of right or wrong. Sin and immorality, as commonly understood mean no more than sexual delinquency in word or act. Anything else is subordinated to a peripheral significance. This exclusive encroachment of meaning on these two terms, means that Christianity, in the eyes of the majority, fulfils little more than a policing function of sexual mores.

This, of course, is bad news for morality or ethics within its broader framework. The church, therefore, fails to exert its moral pressure on the other six deadly sins of covetousness, anger, gluttony, envy and sloth, to anything like the degree of its pressure on those who contravene the sexual code, or indulge in lust. Is it, then, any wonder that our own society is so very corrupt and rotten, when the church in practice, enforces such a narrow view of morality?

10 – Some sexual issues for consideration

In turning directly to the question of sexual mores, church leaders might profitably seek out answers to the following questions so that such answers are not only in alignment with correct ethical thinking, but also with those of psychology, medicine and physiology – i.e. in meeting the demands of a perfectly functioning human being experiencing a minimum of conflict between mind and body. The initial response of church leaders to the above requirement, however, will be that man is uniquely cursed by such a conflict. But our argument is that this inner conflict has reached a degree which is so intolerable and pathological, as in practice to destroy the possibility of living a truly ethical life.   That is, sexual repression arising from this conflict, is sublimated into the ills of aggression, cruelty, and all manner of perversions preventing the achievement of the good life. The pressing question therefore arises: Should these mores be retained, or should they be altered in better suiting the needs of human nature?

The following are some questions offered for debate: 1. Is the sexual instinct a sin, and if so, how can such a thesis be maintained on the grounds outlined above?   2. Are erotic thoughts sinful, and if so, within what contexts? 3. Is an erection at the sight of an attractive woman (other than a properly married wife), or an erection at the sight of a page-3 girl in the *Sun* a mortal sin?   It is certainly so in the eyes of traditional Christian theology, even though the churches may have subsequently revised their thinking on this. But any such revision of thinking has not sunk through to the consciousness of the ordinary man, for in regard to the precepts of religion (although not in regard to commonsense) he still experiences a sense of sin in response to such physiological stimuli.

The fact that his commonsense will nonetheless contemptuously push aside the sense of sin is no evidence that the latter is still not hovering in the background.   4. Is pleasure, experienced during sexual intercourse, to be regarded as either a sin or a curse? 5. Is sexual stimulation by either partner towards the other a sin? 6. Does the sex act become more ethically justifiable if it is undertaken without pleasure? 7. If there is an affirmative answer to the above, should a man therefore seek out a wife with the least possible sex appeal? This question is particularly relevant in view of the fact that mothers are often very partial to advising their sons against associating with women with exceptional sex appeal. 8. Should any rules, barring defined perversion, constrain the performance of sexual intercourse? It should be noted that the Islamic and Jewish religions have stringent regulations for the performance of the sex act. Whilst the Moslem is only supposed to enter the woman from the rear, the Orthodox Jew is only permitted to perform the sex act when a sheet entirely divides the couple apart from a small hole allowing for penetration. 9. Does celibacy, motivated by the renunciation of all material pleasure, place a person nearer to God?

10. Is the perusal or reading of pornographic literature a sin, or may it be justified in overcoming impotency? 11. Is the relation or listening to sexual humour or innuendo a sin? 12. Is sexual intercourse outside marriage justified, and if so, under what circumstances? 13. If a couple's marriage is threatened through a man's impotence with his wife, may he without sin have intercourse with another woman so that he becomes more partial to his wife, so saving the marriage? 14. May partners to a marriage, by mutual consent, enjoy a sexual relationship with other partners, if thereby they feel it contributes to the benefit of their own marriage? 15. Which is the lesser evil: the break-up of a marriage with its upset to the children, or the adoption of lovers by the partners to that marriage so that the latter may be saved? 16. Is sex without love amongst the unmarried a sin? 17. Is sex without love within marriage a sin, or is it a duty, or is the question an irrelevance.

11 – Issues not considered

The above ethical issues on matters of sex are central to contemporary problems of their nature, but they do not reflect the more popular issues of their kind. I have not attempted to list any questions with reference to Gays or Lesbians, not only because these are not mainstream issues affecting the majority, but because homosexuality in almost all cultures is regarded as an aberration or unnatural condition. This is not to suggest, however, that it should not be treated with sympathy and understanding. The punitive laws that used to exist in Western Europe against this condition were undoubtedly a disgrace to humanity.

12 – Some proposals on approaching sexual issues

If the church's attitude to mainstream sexual questions is ethically deficient on the grounds of its unrealism or hypocrisy, and because greater ills are allowed to flourish thereby instead (e.g. violence, misery and perversion), then what guidelines are called for? Space forbids anything like a full consideration of the issues, but the following points may be borne in mind in maintaining openness and truth in conjunction with high ethical principles: 1. In the cause of avoiding ambiguity and misunderstanding, the church must courageously establish firm principles on major sexual issues. 2. In maintaining the truth and the authority of newly established principles, the church must insist on an openness of relationships whenever they affect the parties concerned. I.e. if a man or a woman, in saving a marriage, is to have a sexual relationship with another partner, then it should not be done in secrecy from the other spouse, and such an arrangement should be acknowledged by the couple's spiritual adviser. 3. No situation should be allowed to occur which hurts the feelings of either party in a marriage.

Hence priestly authority, and well grounded ethical principles, should be cited in smoothing the way for establishing special arrangements within marriage. 4. No sexual relationships should be deemed desirable if they, a) hurt the feelings, or, b) damage the interests or health of either party. This means that secret affairs, if one party to such a relationship already has a lover (irrespective of whether or not that person is married) should be deemed immoral. It also means that sexual acts between unmarried persons should be protected by contraception and other hygienic precautions. 5. The breaking of sexual relationships between the unmarried, or the desire of one party to develop a relationship with an alternative partner, should be undertaken through special formalities for the purpose in saving the feelings of the hurt party. The failure to perform such necessary formalities should be deemed an immoral transgression. 6. On the first intimations of homosexuality, an individual should statutorily be obliged to seek medical and psychiatric advice for diagnosis and treatment.

If the homosexuality is deemed to be irreversible on either hormonal or psychiatric grounds, the individual should voluntarily register him- or herself as homosexual, so that he or she may, a) be put into contact with relevant associations, and, b) be fully integrated into society, in enjoying all its rights, without the risk of discrimination because of sexual orientation. 7. All pornography should be phased out (including page-3 girls from tabloids) from general retail outlets, and confined to special Therapeutic Salons, to be opened in all towns and population centres.

Such Therapeutic Salons should be owned and managed by medical practitioners (licensed by the state) with on-site advisers. A wide display of soft and hard porn, and other sexual aids, should be available for hire or sale. Only pornography displaying perversion, e.g. bestiality or paedophilia, etc., should be placed under a total ban. The reasons for the general ban on pornography should be, a) so that the public are not offended by the indecency of its distraction when for the greater part of the day they wish to concentrate on other matters, and, b) because its presence is undesirable for children. 8. Separate Therapeutic Salons should be established for Gays and Lesbians, so that heterosexuals may not be offended by the presence of homosexual material.

13 – Utilising love in confronting racism

It may also be observed that there are certain life situations when spiritual advisers might be performing a benefit to the community by actually promoting sexual activity. One of the major evils of our time is racism and racial discrimination. It is probable that the Race Relations Act in certain aspects, exacerbates rather than diminishes this sociological problem. This is because its purely negative and punitive demands tend to push the real issues of racism under the carpet, for those real issues are *only* concerned with the love for our neighbour.

If the churches wished to take effective pro-active measures against the evils of racism, they might do well by identifying racist elements in society and discreetly arranging liaisons between individuals of different groups. If, for example, stone throwing thugs were paired with sexually experienced women of other races, so that a high degree of pleasure was experienced by the consenting parties, the problem of racism might quickly disappear from our streets.

This is because the thugs would undergo a transformation in both their sexual attitudes and their perception of the victimised races. An attraction and growing respect would develop, finally culminating in a general love for the races which were formerly subjected to persecution. It is not suggested that church leaders should necessarily encourage miscegenation or permanent unions, but only sexual relationships that are sufficiently satisfactory to transform the perception of the victimised races in the eyes of former persecutors. Such psychic cures, of course, would only be viable for those of normal sexuality, but hopefully, only a small percentage of racist thugs would fail to fall into such a category. This partial answer to the race problem is concerned with utilising the instrument of love on a realistic basis, and the broadcasting of love should be the first preoccupation of all religious denominations.

Some churchmen, with more conventional views, may defensively respond that they are concerned with Platonic and not with physical love. Such a response, however, would be a vain attempt to escape from the facts as we find them. This is because, in this context, in reality there is no clear division between the Spiritual and the Material. Psychology has clearly demonstrated that the sacred soul in every one of us has been formed by the sexual experiences of our earliest years. Therefore it must be the duty of religious leaders in the future, to utilise physical needs in helping create a society with the highest ideals of spiritual love.

14 – Putting an end to secrecy and hypocrisy

As may be seen, the above proposals are intended to clear away the secrecy and hypocrisy surrounding sexual issues at the present day. Secrecy and hypocrisy are always reprehensible, since they reflect both deceit and guilt, and few acts committed with a sense of guilt are ethically sound. Furthermore, secrecy and hypocrisy are also reflections of psychological frustration or inner conflict, and so again, is psychically undesirable. It can now be seen that the current attitudes of the church towards sexual issues are at best confused, and at worst, deficient in ethical purpose.

The value of the above proposals, although they may be startling on a first reading, is that they promote a more open approach to what are now perceived as often insoluble problems. They also recognise certain situations which have always existed, and always will, because of the nature of human interaction, but they put these situations into a more humane framework to facilitate their social acceptability. And because the approach is open, the way is clear for frank discussion on specific situations which arise, and the formulation of firmly-based general principles and practices. With the achievement of the latter, time alone will ensure that both principles and practice are endorsed by custom as the rule of ethical considerations.

15 – The Christian activist's attitude to sex

Before finally parting from this topic, it would be relevant
to contrast the attitude of Christian enthusiasts to sexual matters
with that of the ordinary population, for it clearly demonstrates
the embarrassment of the former when faced by the general
opinion of society. The Christian enthusiast today attempts to
play down any priggishness he might have betrayed in an earlier
era but he is only partly successful in this. He still self-
consciously abstains from laughing at sexual innuendo or the
kind of jokes which are heard in the Public bar, and he
disdainfully averts his glance from the top shelf at the
newsagents, and gently chides the colleague at work with his
copy of the *Daily Sport*.

He is awkward when he stands with his mug of beer,
amongst the lads, seeming only to await the opportunity to offer a
Christian message; but when he does come out with a remark to
"prove the common touch," his listeners stand silent, aghast at
what is judged as "vulgarity" solely on the grounds that it is so
"out of character." This illustrates the pitiable dilemma of the
Christian enthusiast that after all he remains an "outsider" and is
not really "one of the boys." Sadly, there is little he can do to
alter this perception in the eyes of the ordinary man until the
sexual ethics of religion themselves are changed. The
separateness of the Christian enthusiast from the rest of the
community is even more evident within the environment of his
own church community, where there is an incestuously cosy
atmosphere of mutual support for prejudices held. The walls of
his defence against the realities of the outer world become most
evident through the Parish magazine.

Here the obsession with sexual issues is paramount. There
are prayers against pornography; articles on the dangers of the
"Sexual jungle;" games and Bible evenings for teenagers to keep
them out of the town centre; segregated meetings for men and
women (as if they mistrusted themselves in mixing together); and
charitable appeals for religious literature to be sent to "fallen
women." All these activities are carried out in a kind of frenzied

fear of encroaching sexual chaos, and a prurient interest in sin wherever it may be sniffed down to its source.

Although every intention is good, the motives, actions, and panacea all give rise to questionable psychological origins. There is an urgent need to re-think through the entire theology of sexual life in planning for the future. All values call for a re-valuation in the name of truth. If the proposals made in this chapter were publicly aired by the churches, I believe the latter would regain substantial credibility with the majority of non-churchgoing people.

CHAPTER 12
Immorality of Hellfire Crusading

"Not hate and love, but fear and love are the basic feelings of religion."

Oswald Spengler, *The Decline of The West*, A,Knopf, NY, 1947 ed., Vol. II, p. 265.

1 – Questionable tactics of Hellfire Crusading

Truth is what religion is all about – or should be. As a churchgoer, just a few years back, there was a short period when I was almost pushed into the arms of ardent atheism. This was following a week-long evangelical crusade.

There was a build-up of many months before the fateful week, during which all the Christian churches played a part. As preachers of some note had been invited to participate during the week-long crusade with its colourful nightly events in different locations, I looked forward with some anticipation to the approaching festival. My hopes, however, were not to be fulfilled.

By the end of the week, I felt the entire episode had been a fraud on the public. Its crusading techniques were those of the multi-national pushing out fast moving consumer goods – only less honest and far more ruthless. Every night, in a large church, was a fine sing-song culminating in an address appealing for commitment then and there. But instead of reasoned arguments there were threats, or falsely-reasoned arguments, or narratives of subjective experience – but always followed by threats.

2 – Its repudiation of the truth

One evening, a "qualified philosopher" addressed the huge congregation – or so he described himself – and he proceeded to immediately abuse the intellectual integrity for which he was responsible as a trained professional. At the close of his talk – like the rest – he pondered on the consequences of failure to take up the challenge, and on the nature of Hell. Although he was not quite sure of the characteristic features of Hell (he stopped at the idea of describing the heat and flames) he assured his congregation that it did nonetheless really exist. As he descended from the pulpit, to the grandeur of the organ, some four or five elderly women, out of a congregation of 700, hobbled slowly towards the altar, to be pounced upon by a crew of eagle-eyed scavengers, who hurried them away to a private corner where they might seize hold of their eternal souls.

By the end of the crusade I was not alone in my feelings of disgust at what had passed the previous week. A neighbour and retired civil servant, who had also participated in the events, expressed identical views when I talked with him across the fence. What was most appalling about this evangelical jamboree? It was its repudiation of the truth. It was its drug-like infested emotionalism; the irrationalism of its crowd psychology; the self-congratulatory sense of superiority; and worst of all, its need for threats in attempting to achieve its ultimate purpose. If it was promoting the greatest cause of all time, and the world's greatest religion, then why did it need to use the threat of Hellfire? Was that after all the strongest argument in promoting the Christian message? Were there no better arguments to effect conversion?

3 – Hellfire as the ultimate weapon

Does the use of fear prove any benefits? None except the avoidance of hellfire itself! Then why play the bully with the instrument of fear? No one wants to bow to the threats of the bully. What kind of religion is it that has to stoop to the use of such tawdry tactics? Surely not one recommendable to the seeker after true enlightenment! What kind of image does Christianity present to the great religions of the East if that is its final word? - if you won't have me, then go and get damned! What if Confucianism or Buddhism were to threaten their adherents with hellfire – or worse still, have the incivility to threaten the unconverted? The idea is not only inconceivable but absurdly comical. The entire evangelical crusade had not only been a betrayal of the truth but an episode grossly unethical in its execution from start to finish.

4 – The need for demonstrable truth

Why is truth – i.e. *real* truth, which is demonstrable and able to stand up to the intellectual rigours of modern thought – so important? It is not necessary here to define the philosophical bases of truth – we have already touched on this in Chapter 10, and found that it may be reached in one of several ways. Now the theologian will argue that there is truth in one situation but not in another, and he falsely uses this as a valid excuse for all kinds of assertions and intellectual skulduggery which can neither be demonstrated nor are convincing to the ordinary man.

The theologian, after indulging in the luxury of abstruse metaphysics, which is nothing more than pretentious word-play used as a kind of priestly power or magic to impress the multitude, finally resorts (when all else fails) to the doctrine of Revelation or Faith. Now there is nothing against faith (which is the glorification of trust), for as we have already noted, faith is essential to religion, but it is a valid question to enquire into the issues of that faith.

5 – Failure of theological metaphysics

If standards of truth are maintained, then Revelation as now understood, makes all the abstruse metaphysics and pretentious intellectuality of theology not only unnecessary but seemingly fraudulent. This is because of the far-fetched claims of the assertions made, i.e. the facts alleged to be truths around which theologians have so cleverly spun such elaborate doctrines. Many church leaders today will not even quarrel with the above – in fact, will endorse it.

Being modern, many will dismiss all or most theological metaphysics on the grounds of its intellectual unacceptability to modern men and women, and will simply adopt a fundamentalist, or some other approach, in arguing that faith alone has meaning.

This, of course, distances such churchmen even further away from real truth, for in taking such a stance, they cut themselves away from the last shreds of intellectual or demonstrable proof. Their religion then becomes little more than a subjective experience, based only on intuition and emotion.

6 – Subjective "truth" is not truth

This subjectivity is the meaning of "truth" to the convert today, but because of contemporary knowledge of the mind and the psyche, he not only stands naked in the modern world, but moreover, accused of dishonesty or self-deception. And since the kind of knowledge we are talking about is freely available to anyone of average intelligence, he may also stand accused of failing to inform himself on matters of common knowledge. The charge of dishonesty breaks down into three parts: firstly, on grounds of failing to look into his own mind and analyse the psychological reasons as to why he asserts certain facts to be true; secondly, on the grounds that in view of objective reasoning and knowledge the asserted facts cannot be accepted as true; and thirdly, and most significantly, on the grounds of spreading assertions that he knows to be untrue.

In earlier times, i.e. before Darwin, T.H. Huxley, Freud, Jung, Adler, etc., such assertions of dishonesty would not have had the validity they have today because there was not then sufficient knowledge for the ordinary man or woman to repudiate the assertions made. Today, however, no such exculpation is acceptable. Everyone is responsible for self-information in maintaining truth as a value in itself. The platitude that every man has the right to his own opinion is not entirely true, for in the realm of ethics, no man has the right to believe falsehood in defiance of factual knowledge.

7 – Ethics demands the truth

The above reasons for insisting on the importance of truth are based on the argument that it is wrong to lie, and equally wrong to self-deceive. Lying and self-deception are clearly unethical. But there are other reasons for insisting that demonstrable truth should always be maintained. It is especially wrong in matters concerned with ultimate values, or with religious organisations promoting such values, that any standards less than the most rigorous should be maintained with regard to truth.

It is no argument for the truth, to evoke the Jesuitical approach, that as the ends (or purpose) of the church are the highest, then the means employed in proselytising may be something less than honest. And neither may the more modern (or pragmatic) argument be evoked that since the church is involved in good practical works, then it is excusable to forego the truth in matters of doctrine and faith. It may be expedient to forego the truth in such latter circumstances – it may satisfy the demands of the philosophical pragmatist with regard to the truth – but it is still not the truth appreciated as an intrinsic value and neither is it the realisation of truth.

8 – Only in religion is it seen as necessary to deceive

The strongest arguments for the necessity of maintaining demonstrable truth in religious matters stems from psychological considerations and their ethical outcome. If it is permitted to economise with the truth on matters concerned with ultimate values, then there is an inescapable implication that in some circumstances, it is also allowable in other matters of theoretical dispute. The significance of this and the huge consequences stemming from the situation cannot be over-emphasised: viz., that religion is the sole topic in the cosmos over which men and women feel there is a necessity to deceive (and actually engage in this) when faced by the option of pursuing the demonstrable truth.

There are other spheres of knowledge that are inexact in their nature, e.g. politics, which is riven by dishonesty of every kind, but however gross the construction of such deceits in these secular matters, no attempt is ever made to assert facts that defy the credulity of human knowledge or experience.   The parliamentary statesmen, for example, does not declare in the House that an Angel appeared to him the previous night with orders from on High to increase Corporation tax by 5%; and neither does the humbler politician threaten the electorate that if his party is not returned to power, the nation will be engulfed in an earthquake. If politicians resorted to the "marvellous" or the miraculous, they would simply be locked away in an asylum and forgotten.

9 – Harmful effects of this

Dishonesty in matters of religion has a profound effect on the community in all its attitudes and actions throughout the course of life. This is because religion is instilled from a very early age, both in home and at school. The small child soon comes to realise that he is expected to believe things that are clearly untrue. By the age of seven or eight, he is sufficiently aware of reality, to know that Job could not possibly have been swallowed by a whale and then spewed up unharmed onto a beach three days later. But being a "good" child, he goes along with the story without questioning its actuality. This is his first lesson in hypocrisy and deceit. Likewise, he chooses to believe in Father Christmas, and after several years, reverses the deceit originally imposed by his parents.

As very great numbers of assertions are forced upon him which he is told to accept as factual truths, he is eventually led to rationalise the justification that if adults are allowed to lie to him, then it cannot be too bad a wrongdoing if he lies to others as the opportunity occurs. Children hate to be lied to, especially when it insults their intelligence, but they cannot express this dislike in so many words to adults. They have their own methods of revolt against this imposition of falsehood: amongst small boys it often takes the form of reducing Biblical characters to scurrilous parody and verse. As a 9-year old at an Anglican boarding school, I remember that behind the back of teachers and other adult supervisors and spies, a group of us organised theatricals during which Biblical texts and characters were not merely ridiculed but made the subject of gross obscenities. The theatricals were hugely popular and met with loud applause and laughter. This was our secret revenge for having to attend three interminable church services every Sunday. It was a healthy response to the psychological oppression of deceit or the imposition of useless knowledge.

10 – Adverse effects of the Bible on the unbeliever

Another harmful aspect stemming from failure to maintain the highest standards of demonstrable truth, is that it leads to sloppy modes of thinking in all those situations where theoretical reasoning power is needed. The critical sense is diminished on exposure to persuaders, hidden and overt, of every conceivable kind, from corrupt politicians to the purveyors of shoddy goods and services. The crudity of the Bible, with its black and white situations and its violent resolution of problems, coarsens the mind of the unreligious, so that the subtleties and complexities of real life are submerged under a grey fog. The unconscious influences which then come to bear on the unbeliever, are calls for the return of flogging or hanging, and vindictive attitudes towards perceived opponents of every kind. As attitudes to right and wrong stem from a very early age, it is not surprising that Biblical teaching in this context often retains its hidden and harmful life-long influence.

It is important to consider the ethical effects of the Bible on the unbeliever, for here it exerts a greater social influence on society as a whole than on the believer. This is simply because only the tiniest proportion of the population exposed to the Bible, are in fact believers. The majority only have the book pushed under their noses in early childhood, and although they may reject its teaching on reaching adulthood, it has nonetheless impressed its unconscious life-long mark for good and ill.

If the majority therefore believe that the God they have been taught to believe in is not loving, benevolent and most merciful, but on the contrary, a vindictive and prurient old man whose primary consideration is the condemnation of sexual pleasure as sin, then that is a significant factor of popular belief.

Of course, in reality, a significant proportion of that majority will form their own impression of a different God, but it is rare for this alone to attract them back to the Bible or to serious Christian belief.

CHAPTER 13
The Search for Religious Belief

"Intellectual indoctrination without emotional excitement is remarkably ineffective, as the empty pews of most English churches prove."

William Sargant, *Battle For The Mind*, Heinemann, 1957,
p. 98.

1 – Philistinism of the contemporary church in comparison with the Victorian era

The most damning influence of conventional religion on the cause of demonstrable truth is undoubtedly through the denigration of the rational instinct by religious leaders. And because of the declining significance of doctrine in favour of faith, there is a rising chorus of revolt against reason in all its forms.

Of course the revolt against reason cannot be blamed solely on the churches: it is, unfortunately, part of the intellectual climate in which we live.[84] But the contemporary churches cannot entirely escape blame for an intellectual philistinism and vulgarity, that they never had 100 years ago, in the cultural environment of Benjamin Jowett, Henry Hart Milman, William Stubbs and Richard Green. During the Victorian era, not only did churchmen aspire to the highest ethical standards, but ranked amongst their number some of the finest minds of the period, who would never have lapsed below the most stringent demands of demonstrable truth – even if occasionally they risked controversy in the church, as occurred with Milman early in his career. These were giants amongst men! It is difficult to find men of such learning and integrity amongst churchmen today.

---

[84] See Part IV of, *The Foundations of New Socialism*, for a detailed discussion on the revolt against reason.

2 – A churchman's dismissal of ethics

Some years ago I was in discussion with a clergyman on the subject of ethics, and tried to impress upon him the importance of studying John Rawls' topical and important book, *A Theory of Justice*. He had the presumption to dismiss the entire subject matter of ethics as "impractical" and not worth the study, insisting that revelation and the Bible alone had any meaning. Such a defiant glorification of ignorance is an appalling indictment of the church. The reality is that world problems cannot possibly be approached without a serious consideration of ethics.

It is a sad commentary on the Christian churches that their own leaders are heralding the demise of religion through failing to face reality and uphold the truth. And it is a fact of existence that in the truth of a thing is to be found the binding and only quality for its meaning. Such, then, is the importance of truth!

3 – Value of the churches in arousing social consciousness

Before parting finally from a discussion of truth, we must redress the balance of one aspect of the topic considered above. There has been no intention to suggest that the influence of the churches on their members is entirely negative – even though at best it may not entail a proper enlightenment most desirable in any life situation.

The greatest value of the churches to their members, especially with regard to the Roman Catholic and Free churches, is that they stimulate a consciousness of the universality of humankind within our global village, and of the foibles, faults, and helplessness of man; and at the hour of death, his equality before God. This, in turn, arouses a social consciousness and the need to affect good works on earth for the benefit of humankind. However prudish or arrogant – even sometimes inhuman – the born again Christian may sometimes appear, it cannot be denied that he has a benevolence of attitude towards his fellow beings, which he is prepared to express in action, transcending all ideological motives of a purely political nature.

This benevolence, therefore, is founded on an objective love of God, and because it is less subjective than political motivation, it stands on a sounder ethical basis. This sensitivity and benevolence is not always reflected to such a strong degree, unfortunately, amongst members of the Anglican Church. This is because the latter is too often seen as an organ of the establishment, and its congregations are in great part made up by those who feel they maintain – or improve – their social standing through regular church attendance. There is too great an emphasis on prayers for the government and its ministers, and all those with power and privilege; and too little thought for the humble and oppressed. Although the Church of England has many clerics of high moral renown, it is not without some truth referred to as the "Tory party at prayer."

4 – And as a haven for the unfortunate

The churches also perform another positive function of social value. This is a psychological role for the benefit of certain sectors of people, who without it might otherwise find themselves seriously adrift. Amongst born again Christians of every fair-sized church congregation, are to be found an assortment of psychopaths, ex-drug addicts, alcoholics, gamblers, pederasts, and old lags, etc. These people usually blend unnoticeably into the main body of the congregation, but observing them aside, they usually convey an appearance of humility and self-effacement, as if they had been broken on the wheel of life.

They seem at the same time defeated and stoical, and yet take them aside, and they will gladly admit to being "Slaves of Christ!" It is difficult to conclude as to whether they really benefit from church membership, or on the contrary, are only exploited by it. Commitment to Christ, after a personal tragedy or crisis in life, does not necessarily mean a person has recovered his full humanity or balance, particularly if there is a self-

imposed asceticism and a denial of the material world. Within
the context of being considered a social problem, i.e. in the eyes
of social workers, drug and alcohol treatment centres,
magistrates, the police and prison warders, their church
membership may be welcomed as a benefit to the community.
Hence, for the lack of an alternative organisation, offering a
better refuge, the value of the churches must be acknowledged for
the role they perform in satisfying an inner need for great
numbers of unfortunates in the community.

5 – Bible most significant as a study in resentment

If in the foregoing there has seemed to be a criticism of the
Bible *per se*, then this was never intended. The criticism has
been directed solely at the effects of the Bible used as revelation.
The Bible is undoubtedly one of the greatest – if not the greatest
book, tracing the ethical evolution of a primitive people. It is a
book of unique and extraordinary interest in tracing the
sociological development of ancient tribes, and numerous
passages may be placed amongst the greatest literature and poetry
of the world.

Its main interest lies in its moral fervour and the psychology
that brought this about. It embraces the engrossing history of a
people pushed around and oppressed by stronger neighbours, and
the entire book amounts to a psychological study of resentment
and hatred because of this. The personality of God, and his
actions, mirrors the wish-fulfilment of the Jewish people in their
despair and struggle against indomitable odds. The final section
of the Bible, the Book of Revelation, summarises the spirit of the
whole, for it culminates in a magnificent crescendo of hatred and
resentment, not only implicitly against the Roman emperor, Nero,
but against the mood and art of classical civilisation.[85] It is a
grand summation to a theme maintained in drama and thought
throughout several millions of words. The Bible chronicles the
struggle for the achievement of freedom in any realisable form.

---

[85] For an elaboration of this interpretation of the Book of Revelation, see Ernest Renan's *The
Antichrist* (being the 4th volume of his great classic, *Les Origines de la Christianisme*), Eng.
trans. published by Walter Scott, 1899.

The main thread of its ethical teaching is to be found in this struggle for freedom and in that is to be found its relevance for modern man with his moral evolutionary outlook.

6 – In this light it is a work of aesthetic truth

If the Bible is studied in this light, it will always prove a source of interest and enlightenment – even of spiritual inspiration and catharsis, as with any great work of art. In these contexts, the Bible may be seen as a work of aesthetic truth – but it is strictly a book for adult reading. It is wrong to read into the Bible anything more than its aesthetic function through which frequently ethical conclusions may be drawn with care. The Bible should not be seen as a work inspired by God, for as we shall demonstrate in the following chapter, this would amount to blaspheming the name of God. The Bible is purely a work of the fallible human mind, and in that is to be found its interest. To regard and use the Bible as revelation, is to degrade its value to the status of a magic formulary. Its ethical truth is thereby diminished by transposing values from one historical era to another, so giving rise to interpretations that were never originally intended.

7 – Truth is sacrificed when the Bible is used as Revelation

Those preachers who urge on their congregations to "lose" themselves in the Bible are the worst of all in this context of misinterpreters since they advance an approach of extreme subjectivity and emotionalism in creating the widest divergence possible between textual or semantic meaning, and comprehension as formulated in the mind of the recipient. When the Bible is put on such a pedestal as to be a sacred text or God's word, and is to be held in the awe of infallibility, it is put beyond the reach of objective consideration for intelligent discussion.

That is, it is not allowed to be seen in the critical light as a human product, and consequently, it is read and used purely as a definitive and oracular authority against which no counter response is permitted. Such an abuse of the Bible amounts to the use of the cudgel and the closing down of the intellect. "Just bathe your mind in the words and soak up the message,!" is the meaningless reiteration of churchmen and churchwomen everywhere when the message itself goes unexplained in terms of realistic analysis. It is a dangerous exhortation – dangerous not merely to demonstrable truth, but as we shall see in the next chapter, dangerous to the cause of religion established on its soundest ethical basis.

8 – And to deny the spiritual truths of other religions

Coterminous with the insistence on taking the Bible as a sacred text, is the refusal of Christians to use prayers, invocations, hymns, etc., from non-Judaeo-Christian sources, on the spurious grounds that such material is invalid for proper use as spiritual inspiration. There is an arrogance in this exclusion stemming from the exaggerated degree of awe placed on the recognised sacred works. So, for example, prayers or songs, often of great poetic beauty, from the cultures of pagan or other religions, are denounced as works of the "Antichrist" or the "Devil," or by some other such emotive and nonsensical description.

It is simply not permitted that they should be considered on their literary merits and then introduced into a Christian service, in the superstitious fear that that service might somehow be defiled and the Lord's name blasphemed. This, of course, is no help towards the cause of a wider ecumenicalism to include all the peoples of the world in their own particular expression of goodwill.

9 – No book exclusively promotes the spiritual truth

No sacred text holds the world monopoly of spiritual values. Some of the most powerfully spiritual books in the world are neither of a sacred nor even of an overtly religious nature. Many of the novels and short stories of Dostoevsky undoubtedly fall into this category, and in conjunction with their profound psychological insight, they express the highest ethical ideals within the religious context. The same may be said of the later works of Tolstoy – especially his novel, *Resurrection*. The heart of the ordinary man or woman may more easily be touched by the striking relevance of the stories of Dostoevsky, Tolstoy, or Charles Dickens (note, *The Christmas Carol*), than by a casual reading of the Bible which is so far removed from the experiences with which the ordinary man or woman can identify.

10 – All religions must be subjected to sociological analysis

Humankind needs the spiritual fulfilment of religion in the same way that he needs bodily sustenance. All cultures have embraced religions of one kind or another – even Palaeolithic man – and these religions have varied in the degree to which their influence has been for good or ill on society. When religions come to dominate society in such a way that they act as a bar to technological or philosophical progress for the improvement of society, they then become decadent. This usually occurs when technology and thought outpaces the traditional religion of a society.[86] That is the reason why all religions should be subjected to sociological analysis, for a religion that has outgrown its function, or becomes decadent, soon loses its ethical value. It is a paradox that whilst all religions regard their values as unchanging and eternal at any one point in time, this is very far from being so in fact.

11 – Criteria for measuring the decadence of a church

There are five criteria by which the decadence of a religion may be assessed: 1. The falling away of serious belief by a great proportion of its followers; 2. The collapse of credibility of essential doctrinal beliefs in the eyes of informed men and women; 3. The failure to uphold ultimate ethical values; 4. The

---

[86] The standard work in the English language on Christianity's efforts to retard progress is Andrew D. White's absorbing masterpiece, *A History of The Warfare of Science With Theology In Christendom*, Arco, 1955, 2 Vols. in 1, first published in 1895.

hypocrisy of great numbers of those who support conventional religion; and, 5. The introduction of new doctrines which are antipathetic in an attempt at modernisation. For two hundred years, the decline of religion has given rise to the popular conclusion that man has no need for it. The 19th century materialists, Utilitarians, and others, simply argued that man had outgrown religion. This was a wrong conclusion and is now accepted as such.

12 – Present diversity of religious belief

The search for a satisfactory religion is not only manifested by the atomisation of religion as first triggered by the Reformation, but by the emergence of an infinite variety of pantheistic beliefs. In the latter category, amongst contemporary beliefs, may be cited an almost religious commitment to environmental issues, as organic agriculture, the campaign against nuclear power, self-sustainable communes, neo-druidism, etc. The leaders of these beliefs are often as self-evident in their dress as is the Catholic priest in his cassock. These beliefs, of course, have not yet mutated into full blown religions, but the feeling of common identity, and its intensity on many issues, forms the basis for religious organisation.

13 – "Feminist" Christianity

In the second category, in this search for satisfactory religious belief, especially amongst feminists in Northern Europe, may be cited the desire to include the Apocrypha and Gnostic texts within the main body of the Bible (supposedly suppressed by anti-feminist and homosexual early "fathers" from the 2nd to the 3rd centuries onwards), so that, firstly, women are credited with having performed a more active role in the establishment of Christianity, and secondly, Christ is perceived as more human in his sexuality. There are now growing numbers of women in Germany and Scandinavia, whose belief in Christianity is only upheld by the conviction that Jesus experienced a physical relationship with Mary Magdalene.[87]

The Gnostic and other texts, some of which were only re-discovered in the 20th century, on which these new and controversial beliefs are based, are proving a nightmare to Anglican, Roman Catholic and other church leaders whose doctrinal beliefs are set in a more conventional mould. The re-discovery of religious texts of one kind or another, therefore, cannot be simply suppressed as in the past. The religious instinct will always find its own level in every community, expressing itself in a variety of unexpected, and possibly, undesirable forms.

---

[87] This is confirmed by texts that record the fact that he "kissed Mary Magdalene on the lips many times," and that she had a "special place" in his heart. One of the most popular books propagating what approaches a feminist type of Christianity is Dr. Elisabeth Moltmann-Wendel's, *Ein eigener Mensch werden: Frauen um Jesus*, Gütersloher Verlagshaus, 4th ed., 1984. The author is a Lutheran theologian living in Tübingen – a centre of Protestant controversy. It may also be noted that Gnostic beliefs have exerted a strong influence on German thought since the Reformation. In this context note especially the works of the 17th century Protestant theologian, Gottfried Arnold, also the influence of Gnosticism on Goethe, Novalis and Hegel – not to mention Jung and the Theosophical movement in the 20th century. See also, Elaine Pagel's, *Gnostic Gospels*, Penguin books.

CHAPTER 14
Towards a Rational Theology

"The teaching of Christ, as it appears in the Gospels, has had extraordinarily little to do with the ethics of Christians."

Bertrand Russell, *Why I Am Not A Christian*, Allen & Unwin, 1957, p. 18.

1 – Reasons for the need for true religion

Why does humankind need a true religion, i.e. a belief in God or in a system of ultimate belief which is possibly without a God, as is the case, for example, with Buddhism? Because, in the words of Christopher Dawson, "every living creature must possess some spiritual dynamic, which provides the energy necessary for that sustained social effort which is civilisation."[88] It is also needed by the individual psyche. A religion at its best fulfils the following functions:-

1. As an ultimate standard of values identifying the beneficence of existence, and all that is worthy in the cosmos.

2. As a basis for understanding, love, and good works amongst all humanity, in promoting the motto, "One for all and all for one!"

3. In giving the soundest ethical rationale for the purpose of existence, both to the individual and society.

4. In bringing peace to the soul of the individual in his relationship with the cosmos and society, particularly with regard to ultimate destiny.

5. In the awe that there will always exist the unknowable which is known to God alone (or to the cosmos) until its discovery by man.

---

[88] Dawson, op. cit., p. viii.

2 – The paradox of religious appeal

The above, however, should not be interpreted as a justification for religion, or for any specific religion; but only as a reflection of humanity's need for religion. Religion in itself can only be justified on the grounds of truth, and in our own era, this has to mean demonstrable truth.

The difficulty of achieving this in the present age, however, follows from the following paradox: Whilst the very attraction of the great religions in the Western world is to be found in the mythology of their doctrines, it also acts as a repellent to the rational non-churchgoing majority. The majority (and this also includes churchgoers) enjoy a consciously held hypocrisy which says, "I like to believe what I cannot possibly believe." The truth of this paradox is also reflected in the impossibility of successfully constructing rational religions out of the void of a mere intellectual construct.

Thus, the worship of the Supreme Being during the French Revolution, or Comte's religion, backed by its powerful philosophical synthesis, with its worship of Humanity, the Great Being, and the Earth, all came to nothing. As to what extent the attraction of the mythology of religion may be said to be aesthetic or truly religious (i.e. mystic) it is impossible to say. The fact remains that modern educated men and women cannot easily admit the idea of the supremacy of a non-rational power. In any successful modern religion there has to be a perfect balance between the Intellectual, the Ethical and the Emotional, and it is the Ethical which holds together this balance.

3- Need for a broader ecumenical movement

As the success for inventing a new religion in the vacuum of a non-traditional environment seems impossible, the hope of humanity must be seen in the promotion of an ecumenical movement based on the idea of unity, not merely amongst the Christian churches, but amongst all the major religions of the world, and these may be held together under the umbrella of deism. In this way, such a movement would best be guaranteed from the start a truly religious spirit, as those with the goodwill for all humankind were drawn to its support. In ensuring trust and avoiding the subjectivity of vested interest beliefs, such a movement would need to be organised and led initially by non-churchgoers and religiously inspired deists.

It greatest significance would be seen as an influence on the theological thinking of the different religions themselves. The purpose of such a movement would be to develop general rational principles as to the nature of God, Immortality, Prayer, etc., out of which would eventually evolve a rational world theology and a popular world religion inspired by the principles of deism. Such a religion would inevitably be based on good works since the cooperation of the older churches in the medical and charitable fields would be the most likely factors in cementing a closer and deeper understanding. It would serve as a practical basis of mutual goodwill for dialogue and ever closer links. A strong ethical faith in the need to serve the ultimate interests of humanity would be the overriding spirit of such a religion.

4 – The need for faith and how it works

In view of the foregoing, we may now tentatively propose certain guiding ideas which may be most significant in the life of such a religion. The following concepts, being vital to most true religions, will therefore be briefly presented for discussion: *Faith*; *God*; *Immortality*; *Heaven*; *Hell*; *Forgiveness*, and *Prayer*.

Faith is not only essential to the religious instinct, but is the first step to goodness, for in the context of religion, it is the first recognition of goodness. The life of no being is possible without the existence of faith in some degree. The child trusts the mother that holds it in her arms; the man leaving home for work trusts he will reach his destination; the student trusts he will pass his exams; the woman trusts in the success of her household tasks; the newly-weds trust in their future joy; and most trust, that on balance, their future will be blessed by happiness with a minimum of anxiety and sorrow.

This is the experience of faith on the mundane level. But religious faith requires something more. It entails an optimism transcending the trite experience of ordinary hope. Religious faith should be linked to a rational force perceived as the source of all good; and that force must act as both the inspiration of that faith and as a motive for good works.

That alone constitutes the nature of religious faith but something more is required in the context of its commitment to a true religion. The Communist and the Environmentalist may be said to have a religious faith, if their idealism is sufficient to convince them that Communism or Environmentalism offers humanity an answer to all the questions of the cosmos. Environmentalism has not as yet attempted such an ambitious exposition of its beliefs, but Communism, through the profound philosophy of dialectical and historical materialism, did construct such a cosmic view. Nonetheless Communism was not a religion and it explicitly denied the possibility for such an assertion.

5 – Description of those without faith

The nature of religious faith, as a subjective experience, comes into greater clarity when contrasted with those who are without such faith. The faithless are so often marked by a psychological pessimism, and a cynicism unrelieved by belief in a rational force for the good of humankind. The joyous creativity of the religiously faithful is reflected in their works and deeds. It is inspired by a positive assertion of life. Those without faith express a certain self-destructiveness in their lives, emanating from an un-integrated personality – i.e. un-integrated into the ethical will of the cosmos. They convey a frustration and incompleteness which seems to limit the quality of their lives. When they are elated and the centre of attention or amusement, it is often for their sardonic humour and a hidden cruelty and malice. Their attitude to the world is expedient and self-centred.

Whilst the religiously minded are positive and full of good potential; the irreligious (who should be differentiated from the philosophical atheistic) are negative and full of bad potential.

Nonetheless, as human beings live in a state of flux, there always remains the possibility of conversion, and it is more common for unbelievers to become believers than vice versa.

It should be noted that the above descriptions are of psychological states of mind and behaviour for which the individual very often is not or cannot be held entirely responsible. Furthermore, as should be understood from what has been said earlier in this book, the above descriptions of the religiously faithful and non-faithful cannot necessarily be correlated with the majority of those who actively support the different churches, or otherwise, for church attendance has a wide diversity of motives.

6 – Faith without true religion is sterile

But religious faith in itself (as noted at the start of these chapters) should not be taken as a criterion for good or bad thinking or action.   This is because religious faith does not achieve its highest potential until linked to true religion.   It is nothing more than a force, similar to electricity or nuclear fission, and only becomes supremely good when linked to the beneficent outcome of a true faith.   That is the reason why religiosity should not be taken as a criterion for goodness or nearness to God, for not only are there many false religions, but even true religions can exert an eeriness through their own fanaticism or false aspects.   These things have been demonstrated by history throughout the ages.

7 – The meaning of God

God is the Supreme Being, if Being is understood in its definition as Essence (i.e. spiritual entity), and not as a person or superhuman actor intervening in the affairs of the world. As God is manifest in everything that is good – in every blade of grass and in every act of creativity – it would be meaningless to understand his essence as anything less than the positive force for good, and the act of becoming, i.e. development and potential, and the realisation of potential.   In the words of Prof. Alexander, one of the most important modern exponents on the nature of God, "God as an actual existent is always becoming deity, but never attains it. He is the ideal God in embryo. The ideal when fulfilled ceases to be God."[89] And again, "the infinite God is purely ideal or conceptual. ... As actual, God does not possess the quality of deity but is the universe as tending to that quality."[90]

To perceive God as an independent deity intervening in the events of the world, both good and bad, and as responsible for those events, would not only entail a retardation in the understanding of God but amount to blasphemy. As Christopher Dawson has maintained, "God is not the creator of the world, he is himself created with the world, or rather he 'emerges' as part of the cosmic process."[91] Julian Huxley has rightly argued that, "God can no longer be considered as the controller of the universe in any but a Pickwickian sense. ... God is beginning to resemble not a ruler, but the last fading smile of a cosmic Cheshire cat."[92] Huxley also calls upon churchmen for honesty in their approach to God, when he writes, "for theologians to claim that God is 'in reality' some abstract entity or depersonalised spiritual principle, while in practice their churches inculcate belief in a personal divinity who rules and judges, who demands worship and submission, who is capable of anger and forgiveness – that is plain intellectual dishonesty."[93] This, of course, returns us to the question of the Bible, for if it is to retain its pre-eminent position, how else are our poor clergymen to preach to their congregations?

The idea of a personal intervening God is therefore inexplicable and inconceivable. It might have suited our primitive ancestors who derived their religion from even older sources, and a polytheism of one system or another, but even the whittling down of the gods to a single monotheistic deity is but a small step to the achievement of belief in the true rational God.

---

[89] Prof. Samuel Alexander, *Space, Time & Deity*, Gifford Lectures 1920, Vol. II, p. 365.
[90] Ibid., p. 361.
[91] Dawson, op. cit., p. 239.
[92] Huxley, op. cit., p. 58.
[93] Ibid., p. 49.

If the God of the early Jews was hardly less tribal than Zeus, Jupiter or Odin, then the Christian God of a later era was hardly perceived in a form any less personal or human than the gods of our pagan forebears. And as we have earlier noted, God in human form is a contradiction of his immanent nature. God is only capable of working through man, nature and the cosmos, for in these things lies his omnipotence. As an essence he is unknowable except through the rationality of our religious faith; the good works of nature and humankind; and the ethical evolution of society. In summary, God can only be defined as the coming into being of the potentiality for good. This alone allows us sufficient room for the contemplation of his greatness.

8 – Essential to a modern religious consciousness

Belief in God is essential to the concept and formation of a modern religion with a social message, since recognition of the omnipotence of the Supreme Being is the one factor ensuring the achievement of necessary objectivity. This is simply because he acts as a focus of attention and unity of understanding within the social context. Religiosity, or religious feeling without God is limited in its ability to exert goodness or endorse a permanence of values, since it relies on too subjective a framework for measuring good and evil; or else, as with Buddhism, it concentrates too egoistically on the individual so that the problems of the community are simply swept aside as irrelevant. Buddhism is the one great religion without a god.

Turning in general to other religiously held godless beliefs, these latter tend to be restricted in their understanding, since they fail to take account of the cosmic or universal situation of existence. So, for example, religiously held beliefs in environmentalism or a self-sustainable economy, are not sufficient in themselves to constitute a religion, as they fail to take into account all the conditions of conscious existence affecting the fate of humanity. The same may be said of Communism as witnessed by both its collapse and the intellectual bankruptcy of dialectical materialism.

9 – The impersonality of God

By the same argument, belief in a personal God, or sacred scripts, allegedly expressing the word of God with all their specific commands of both a positive and negative kind, are also limiting in the realisation of true religion for the modern age. This is because such a personal God and such scripts are limited by the subjectivity of their historical context. Commentaries and theological gymnastics are not sufficient in the cause of truth by attempting to transform such subjectivity into objective realism. This is why a new theology and a new understanding of God is so urgently required.

But the supporting arguments for the existence of such a God are far more likely to be found in philosophical writings than in pure theology. Many, for example, have found themselves very much nearer to God, and found greater spiritual inspiration, through reading the writings of Hegel than in any Biblical passage. This is because of Hegel's striving for the Absolute truth, and an objectivity which is so de-personalised as to be God-like in its impression. This is the intellect used for its highest possible purpose.[94] A further reason for the intense spirituality of Hegel was pointed out by Christopher Dawson when he wrote that, "the Hegelian conception of history remains fundamentally religious. It is a philosophy of Incarnation, of the progressive self-manifestation of God in history."[95] Hegel's philosophy gives at the same time a self-respecting dignity and purpose to the life of the individual and society through this manifestation of God.

10 – Taking God's name in vain

If God's name is to be used with respect, then it must be through an understanding of the above exposition. It is therefore an insolence to God, and a fraud on the public, to assume such a

---

[94] F.H. "Bradley maintained that the concept of God is required by the religious consciousness but that, from the philosophical point of view, it must be transformed into the concept of the Absolute," Frederick Copleston, *A History of Philosophy*, Burns & Oates, Vol. VII, p. 25.
[95] Dawson, op. cit., pp. 200-201.

status of self-importance as to claim that God has "called" a person to do this or that action, or was responsible for achieving some mundane desired event. Church magazines are full of such pseudo-reverential phrases. In a 600-word article I recently read, written by an especially elated lay preacher, the phrase "called by God," or by "God's grace," occurred eight times, all in connection with actions which he personally was trying to promote.

Clergymen moving to a new benefice are particularly guilty of this hypocritical cant which is intended to impress parishioners with its pious authority. When a clergyman declares that he has been "called" to take up a particular living, what he really means is that he is bored by the uneventfulness of his old parish, or sickened by the grumbling of the Wives' Fellowship committee, or exasperated by the incompetence of his verger whose sight he can no longer endure, or more often today because he is simply seeking a move and new scenery, as some kind of escape, because his marriage is on the rocks. These explanations, of course, could never be openly expressed, but "called" by God is far too grandiose an excuse for something much more mundane. Every clergyman has only to look into his own heart before realising the real motive for his move, but he should never resort to imposing on his parishioners with what is so clearly untrue.

11 – He is not a mere intervener in fulfilling petty desires

The impersonality of God in his great omnipotence deserves greater respect than reduction to the status of a mere seducer from one benefice to another. The church should show recognition to God, but why should God defer in reciprocating such recognition? Does he hold any special merit in a band of self-appointed worshippers over the rest of humanity? Surely not! An all-merciful and loving God holds all humanity in equal regard. He has no special places for special cases, and certainly cannot prefer one people to another on account of their church, or theology, or evolutionary advance in intellectual and spiritual progress.

The Christian church noted the reality of this theological problem from the earliest centuries of its history. The question was often asked: Should Socrates be condemned to eternal hellfire because he died 300 years before the possibility of receiving Christian baptism? Today the problem is still unresolved, although the churches adopt a more generous attitude towards non-Christian peoples and non-believers at home.

12 – Foolish attempts at proving God's existence

The difficulty of clergymen in proving the existence of God, according to the rules of Christian theology, is not only a major handicap for Christianity, but a nightmare for churchmen themselves. Many years ago as a 9-year old boarder at a Church of England public school, I remember our divinity master, who was also a priest, explaining the nature of God. About thirty of us were seated in the school hall, and our teacher drew a complex geometrical diagram on the blackboard as a proof of God's existence.

The demonstration, to my young mind, seemed silly and unconvincing. No one except me was prepared to question the proof. I was not attempting to be "clever," or to false foot the young divine, but was seeking genuine enlightenment when I took the clergyman up on his own grounds with a simple question on the diagram. I have long forgotten the question and the details of the diagram, but the master hurled the chalk onto the floor and stormed out of the hall in a rage, leaving us boys feeling most embarrassed.

If that is the reaction of the church to honest questions of enquiry, it would do better to leave God out of its theology.[96] The eventual outcome, of course, is that philosophy will take over from theology the task of better describing the nature of God's reality.

---

[96] For modern studies on the nature of God, see especially, Prof. Alexander's, *Space, Time & Deity*, 2 Vols., 1927, Julian Huxley's, *Religion Without Revelation*, Max Parrish, extended 1957 ed.; also, A.N. Whitehead's, *Religion In The Making*, op. cit., pp. 56-62.

CHAPTER 15
Foundations for a Unifying Religion

"It is not enough to point the road along which people have travelled and do travel; the philosopher should also seek to indicate the road along which they ought to travel, precisely because some roads are better than others."

C.E.M. Joad, *Decadence*, Faber & Faber, 1948, p. 25.

1 – The question of Immortality

This immediately leads us into the third concept: that of *Immortality*. Again, this is a term requiring definition, but first it would be apt to glance at immortality within the context of its sociological significance.

Some time ago I was in discussion with a clergyman on the topic of the afterlife, and I contrasted the attitude to death of two great 18th century contemporaries, viz., Dr. Samuel Johnson and David Hume. Whilst Dr. Johnson had a strong religious belief, he was haunted by a life-long fear of death, whilst David Hume, who was an atheist, was fearless in his attitude towards extinction. When Hume was on his death bed, he died cheerful and filled with happiness, and Dr. Johnson on learning about the last hours of the Scottish philosopher, was shocked by what he saw as his levity.[97] I put it to the clergyman that the reasons for Hume's happiness on his death bed, after a long illness, was due firstly, to the recollection of a fulfilled life; secondly, to the fact that he was "approaching as nearly to the idea of a perfectly wise and virtuous man as perhaps the nature of human frailty will permit;"[98] and thirdly, because he was well loved by his friends amongst whom were ministers of religion.

The clergyman, who mistakenly took my story as an implied argument against the need for the idea of immortality,

---

[97] Both Adam Smith and James Boswell have described the dying hours of David Hume. It is only fair to add that Dr. Johnson's mind was happily composed when he met death eight years later.
[98] Letter from Adam Smith to William Strachan of 9th November 1776.

immediately retorted that if there is no afterlife, then life is not worth living.

2 – Bad arguments for its existence

This, of course, is the strongest argument put forward by theologians for the idea of immortality, but it is also the worst reason as to why it should be a fact. It also suggests that not much should or can be done to improve our earthly lot. If life is "not worth living" without the promise of eternal bliss, then it may be assumed that earthly existence must be pretty dreadful.

This attitude reflects a particular view of life: viz., that physical or worldly pleasures should be withheld or deferred in favour of heavenly pleasures to be enjoyed at a future date. But this putting away or investment of present life for the accruing interest and capital enjoyment after the event of death amounts to little more than making a virtue out of sexual repression – and much more besides, as for example, poverty, oppression and misery.

If the promise of immortality is used as an argument to refrain from all acts objectively considered wrongful or criminal, then such a promise remains unethical in its purpose. This is because ethics demands that wrongdoing should be condemned on its own account, and not because it results in such an awful penalty – i.e. descent into the nether world. An ethics based on the promise of immortality is both authoritarian and irrational. Its underlying message repudiates the right to question the why and wherefore of a command. A command is a command because there is no "Why," and the punishment for its transgression is eternal damnation. This is the kind of ethics that can transform any evil into a virtue – even the genocide of a race.

3 – Its usefulness to exploiters and warmongers

On the socio-political plane belief in immortality has an extraordinary usefulness – especially for war-mongering statesmen and governments. If belief in the next world had not been so strongly inculcated into the peoples of Europe, then it is doubtful if so many millions would have so willingly sacrificed their lives in the First World War in the way that they did.

More significant than preparedness for total sacrifice, however, is the usefulness of the idea of immortality to governments who fail to lighten their burden on the poor and downtrodden. The latter may then bathe in the satisfaction that whilst their oppressors will be lost to the underworld, they will be destined to a better future. "The first shall be last, and the last shall be first,!"[99] gives a sweet feeling of satisfaction to the revenge-seeking downtrodden. Such a belief allows generous room for both resentment and hope.

These reasons for believing in an afterlife are also unethical, as well as false in themselves. They are unethical since they not only make use of religion for secret resentment, but because they encourage life-denying attitudes and complacency in the face of injustice.

4 – Heaven as a club for the select few

The traditional Christian doctrines of immortality, and most specifically, the belief that the vast majority are destined to eternal hellfire, whilst only a select minority ascend to heaven, are almost obscene in their inhumanity, and it is surprising how such doctrines are still adhered to (usually by the so-called Free churches) to the present day.[100]

Just a few years ago a 9-year old boy asked his stepmother (an acquaintance of the author) if his natural mother was in heaven or hell. The parents of the child were born again Christians, but the deceased mother and first wife of the father

---

[99] As appears in Matthew xix, 30; Mark x, 31; & Luke xiii, 30.

[100] It should be noted that responsible theologians have denied the existence of Hell from at least the Victorian era. As William Sargant humorously noted, "one of the most important occasions in English religious history may prove to have been when a workman is said to have rushed jubilantly out of a church where Dean Farrar was preaching, and shouted: 'Good news, mates, old Farrar says there's no 'ell!' This could have been about the year 1878, when Farrar published his book, *Eternal Hope*, containing the five sermons he had preached in Westminster Abbey critical of eternal punishment." – William Sargant, op. cit., pp. 130-131.

had been a formal but uncommitted Christian. The stepmother looked at the boy pityingly, and replied that as his natural mother had not openly declared her faith to the congregation, it was not possible to be sure of her whereabouts. All they could do was pray nightly for her soul and hope. Such is an example of the irresponsibility and wicked mischief of the religious minded.

5 – Ethics of the saved and the damned

Modern psychology would argue that as all are victims of the determinism of family and social environment, and as fortune and misfortune fall into a similar category of causation, it would be a gross injustice and unethical to assume a post-mortem division of all humanity into the virtuous and the wicked, and the consequent despatch into heaven or hell. Christian concepts of immortality are both deficient and de-humanising because of the emotive division made between Good and Bad, and the encouragement of "justifiable" vindictiveness, and the tendency to override the need for the analysis of personality.

6 – Better ethics of Eastern immortality

There is far more ethical meaning in the theories of immortality in the religions indigenous to India. Hinduism, Jainism, Buddhism and Sikhism, all uphold a belief in a series of reincarnations to a higher or lower sphere of animal existence, according to the degree of goodness or badness in life. This is a sensible belief, devoid of extreme penalties or rewards (which were never wholly credible to great numbers of people – even during the age of faith), and seems genuinely to encourage its followers along the path of the good life in harmony with the environment. Westerners may look askance at their educated Indian friends as they elaborate on the idea of Karma and the transmigration of souls until their eventual evolution into a state of Nirvana; but Indians may look askance in return at the educated Westerner as he expostulates on the unphilosophical, simplistic and vindictive ideas of the Christian afterlife and its consequences.

It may be asked: Why should man be unique in asking for and anticipating immortality? How can such an erring creature deserve such grace? Is there any logical credibility in the belief in immortality if the rest of the animal kingdom are excluded? Are not dogs, cats and other creatures, showing loyalty and affection, and therefore capable of expressing ethical values, equally deserving a place in heaven? (This returns us to the deficiency of the Abrahamic religions in placing man at the centre of the universe, as the rightful master and exploiter of all he surveys and touches.) Certainly the ancestors of the present Egyptians had a more reverent attitude to the animal kingdom than their Islamic descendants.

There has always been a desire for personal immortality, but the researches of Sir William Osler, who had a wide experience of persons near to death, found that whilst a minority of people ardently desired a future life, another minority hoped for final extinction, whilst the vast majority appeared to be indifferent.[101] The scientist, Ilya Metchnikov, on the other hand, after critically examining the philosophical and religious arguments for immortality, concluded that its belief was due to the unfulfilment of man in the satisfaction of his natural impulses.[102] Hence the conclusions of both Osler and Metchnikov fail to give sufficient reasons as to why it is right to believe in immortality.

7 – A rational definition of immortality

But the question of right in such a context is irrelevant. In this book we are only concerned with demonstrable truth. How can this, then, be made to correspond with a theory of immortality for a new world religious consciousness? Immortality can only be rationally defined as the status of eternal existence conferred by cosmic memory on all that has come into

---

[101] Sir William Osler, *Science & Immortality*, Boston, 1904.
[102] Ilya Metchnikov, *The Nature of Man*, NY, 1903.

being. All that is brought into being achieves a status of reality in terms of time and space, and such a reality repudiates its non-existence. This means that a thing brought into existence cannot be destroyed as an event that was. Cosmic memory is simply the affirmation of the past as fact, and immortality is the spirit of an event in fact which can never lose its eternity.

8 – A definition of Heaven and Hell

This takes us into the definition of *Heaven* and *Hell*. These concepts can only be understood in terms of the ethical consciousness of a dying being. A fulfilled, integrated, or happy personality, may be said to exist in the cosmic memory of benevolence by the fact of goodness alone. An unfulfilled, disturbed or unhappy personality may be said to exist in the cosmic memory of a void until the resolution of that inner conflict through the evolution of the ethical spirit in time and space. Whilst Heaven entails a positive factor in cosmic memory; hell is merely a negative factor, and all that is bad demands eventual resolution into a cosmic order and so return into the essence of the Supreme Being and the idea of the good.

This is because only the good is ultimately real. Whilst the *saved* are those whose memory is preserved in love, the creative bond of the universe; the *damned* are simply the forgotten, the unloved and undeserving until the resolution of their past existence into ethical understanding, which culminates in their ultimate salvation. Thus whilst we may conceive the idea of Heaven in cosmic memory, as only the Good is real; we cannot likewise conceive a Hell, as ultimately, after the resolution of disorder (which is evil) evil has no permanent reality in cosmic existence. We can only conceive the idea of Purgatory, into which the unfortunate may be cast, until the resolution of their wrongs into the ethical understanding of a new order. There is therefore some justification for the medieval concept of Purgatory as formulated by the theology of the Roman Catholic and Eastern Orthodox churches.

9 - Forgiveness

The idea of *Forgiveness*, our sixth concept, is less abstruse than the ideas of Faith, God, Immortality, Heaven or Hell. Forgiveness for transgressions, both intentional and unintentional, and wrong thoughts, may only be achieved by the following steps to contrition: firstly, the subject must achieve a psychological understanding of the causes for his wrongdoing, so that he may take realistic steps towards their correction in the future; and secondly, he must understand the ethical nature of his wrongdoing as an objective fact. Each factor is of little value without the other. Forgiveness then follows contrition and commitment not to re-offend.

Meaningless commands, or commands the rationale of which cannot be comprehended, have a limited validity, often because they have an ulterior motive. Thus the commands of secret societies of a ritualistic nature, are highly suspect since they defy rationality, and the intention of their purposeless discipline is often unethical. Forgiveness for the breaking of such commands is therefore meaningless, as there was no *real* wrongdoing in the first place. The commands of a military-like organisation with a specific social purpose would not, of course, fall into such a category, but the command not to pluck the apple from the tree of knowledge was clearly ulterior, since its purpose was to prevent self-improvement through the acquirement of knowledge as well as protecting the jealously held monopolistic power of a tribal god. Hence the Garden of Eden was merely God's private zoo, holding the threat of a challenge to such a deity through the use of this newly acquired knowledge.

Forgiveness, therefore, is only made possible through an act of enlightenment as a guide to future action and attitudes. The theft of the apple, on the other hand, changed man into an entirely different being in altering his relationship with the cosmos. It was an act for which there could be no forgiveness, and it brought into being the existence of *sin*. The plucking of the apple was in itself no more than an act of petty theft, but it triggered a process transforming the nature of humankind.

Forgiveness is essential at all times between individuals and peoples, wherever there has been wrongdoing, anger or conflict; but the forgiveness of an impersonal omnipotent God is made quietly in the presence of an Absolute ethical being, incapable by his very greatness of resentment or anger. This calls for a process of enlightened self-forgiveness transcending mere contrition. The reality of forgiveness as a sociological factor in society is one of the great contributions of Christianity to Western society. Chinese friends, for example, have assured me that forgiveness is not a characteristic of their own civilisation, and that once an offence is given, it remains as a burning resentment. That is why Confucianism lays such emphasis on form and good manners in avoiding offence in the first place. Many Chinese have been persuaded to adopt Christianity solely on the pragmatic grounds that it allows for forgiveness and mends relationships which might otherwise remain broken forever.

10 - Prayer

The seventh and last concept is that of *Prayer*. As God is a non-intervening deity, as well as an understanding and most merciful being, the act of petitionary prayer would be demeaning to his majesty, since it would give recognition to a magic formulary and thus superstition. Julian Huxley, on the other hand, has written with understanding on the value of contemplative prayer, when he argues that, "all ... other functions of prayer, ... are in reality functions of contemplation and meditation rather than petition. The contemplation may be of some intense desire of the worshippers, such as the desire for purity, and so be cast in the form of a petition; but the psychological machinery will not operate unless the idea permeates the mind. Prayer of this contemplative type is one of the central kernels of developed religion. It permits the bringing before the mind of a world of thought which in most people must inevitably be absent during the occupations of ordinary life: it allows the deepest longings of the soul, driven down below the surface by circumstances, to come into action: and it is the means by which the mind may fix itself upon this or that noble or beautiful or awe-inspiring idea, and so grow to it and come to realise it more fully.   It is thus partly a method of auto-suggestion, partly a means of refreshing the spirit."[103]

This is contemplative prayer at its best, and must not be allowed, as Huxley points out, to degenerate into a ritual of "agreeably familiar words," or be used as an invocation to "exert some mysterious power, or to degrade the soul with thoughts of revenge."

11 – Theology must give way to philosophy

No other concepts need now be discussed in seeking to construct a spiritual, rational, and deistic theology for a unifying world religious consciousness.   Such a consciousness entails a morality based on objective criteria without deception or self-deception.   A minimum of theological ideas have been proposed as a basis for unity in attracting all the great religions towards the unity of an intellectual and spiritual understanding.

The above concepts, and the ideas which have inspired them, may seemingly fall into the category of philosophy rather than theology as strictly understood.   But in the future, the intellectual foundations of religion may increasingly become dependent on the serious discipline of philosophy as opposed to the increasingly worm-eaten support of theological "science."

And here it might be apt to distinguish between these two disciplines and their relationship to religion.   Theology is that intellectual activity primarily concerned with upholding religious doctrines as truths in themselves against all other odds, e.g. the Trinity, the Virgin birth, the nature of the Eucharist, etc.   It should be noted, however, that theology divides up into the following five sectors of interest:- *Natural*: dealing with the knowledge of God as gained from his works by light of nature and reason; *Positive/Revealed*: based on revelation; *Dogmatic*: dealing with the authoritative teaching of the Scriptures and the church; *Speculative*: giving scope to human speculation, not

---

[103]   Huxley, op. cit., pp. 154-155.

confined to revelation; and, *Systematic*: the methodical arrangement of the truths of religion in their natural connection.[104] Nonetheless, despite the breadth of the above definitions, we insist on the greater significance of philosophy in contributing towards modern ideas on religion, simply on the grounds that such ideas have been developed by philosophers and other secular writers, as Dr. S. Alexander, Julian Huxley, A.N. Whitehead, etc. Philosophy is therefore concerned with the more general aspects of religion, stripped of its doctrinal beliefs, e.g. the nature of God, faith, immortality, etc. There are naturally areas where both disciplines may be introduced, e.g. with regard to psychology or the paranormal.

In modern times many learned men (and some women) have turned their minds to theological questions, in utilising the latest researches of philology, archaeology and philosophical thought, in demonstrating doctrinal points. Despite all their courageous efforts, however, theology is becoming increasingly unreadable to the educated public with its rational mind and scientific background. This is simply because some things are un-provable, and the more learning that is used to prove a point, the more dishonesty – or jetsam and flotsam – is heaped onto an issue that is untenable from the beginning. This seems to make the subject matter of theology not so much ridiculous or dull, as disgustingly false in its intellectual gymnastics.

And that is the reason why theology as a living discipline, may need to fall away entirely, in making room for the greater credibility of a philosophy of religion. Theology would then become something of merely historical interest. The necessity for this change of intellectual emphasis in the consideration of religious questions may be read into the words of Julian Huxley when he wrote, "keeping up with the facts is an essential for any enduring idea-system: only by incorporating new facts and new modes of organising knowledge can idea-systems remain effective organs of man in society."[105]

---

104 C.O.D. op. cit., p. 1344.
105 Huxley, op. cit., pp. viii-ix.

It would only be right to add, however, that the notion of the limitations of theology in demonstrating convincing proof is no recent occurrence. Already in the 17th century, the great French religious thinker, Blaise Pascal, bemoaned that, "the metaphysical proofs of God are so apart from man's reason, and so complicated that they are but little striking, and if they are of use to any, it is only during the moment that the demonstration is before them, but an hour afterwards they fear they have been mistaken."[106]

The abstruse metaphysical reasons given for the existence of God, immortality, etc., is yet another reason why we should heed the wisdom of Confucius to "respect the spirits but keep them at a distance." It is more important for man to concentrate on his practical goodness in this world, than to idle his mind on matters to which no intelligent answers may be given. Giving credence to what is not comprehended, or even not comprehensible, is not the path to an honest life. If a world unifying religious consciousness is to have any chance of success, then we must first be honest with ourselves, for if we cannot be honest with ourselves we cannot hope to be honest with one another.

12 – Towards a new religious consciousness

The success of such a unifying religious consciousness would stem from the inoffensive simplicity of its natural theology (or philosophy) arising from its rationality and appeal to sensible men and women worldwide.   Initially it might be weak in spirituality and "enthusiasm" (if the latter may be interpreted in a more positive light) and its theology might appear bland in the eyes of dogmatists, charismatics, and such like people. But as intelligent men and women of goodwill from many cultures worldwide came together, its theology would deepen with the emergence of a new ethical consciousness.

As an organised body, such a church would take on a powerful political role, which whilst eschewing all party political

---

[106]   Blaise Pascal, *Thoughts,* George Bell, Bohn's Standard Library ed., 1890, p. 8.

and vested interest group loyalties, would project its cause as an alternative political force more morally authoritative than that of national governments. In this role it would seek to move the minds of accredited politicians in the striving to create a better and securer world.

The effect of such a political role would be two-fold: firstly, it would reflect a philosophy and policies which in themselves were impregnable, so everywhere attracting those of goodwill; but far more significantly, it would give greater credence to religion itself through the depth of its newly acquired understanding and commitment to substantive political issues, and this in turn would serve as a springboard for the rise of a new religious consciousness. Meanwhile, churchmen themselves, through their learning and grasp of practical matters in society, would regain a status and credibility in the eyes of the public, which they had not enjoyed since the Victorian era.

It is not necessary to anticipate the structure of such an overarching church on the local level, except to remark that it would take the form of groups coming together to listen to talks and participate in discussions on all manner of individual and social problems within their ethical context. The striving towards objectivity and factual knowledge would be the criteria for judging right and wrong. Ceremony would be kept to a minimum, but formal standards would evolve, in facilitating friendship and ease in the conduct of meetings.

A positive attitude would be adopted towards all existing religions and their memberships, in attempts to develop dialogue and cooperation. Whilst different theologies may be regarded with askance by the new believers, the good practical work of all churches would be supported by the new faith. Whilst the sensibilities of the religious of all faiths would be respected, the eventual hope would be the gradual fading away of the older religions as the unifying purpose of the new faith achieved its ultimate purpose for justice and world peace. None can doubt the need for such a movement in a world facing the threat of environmental Armageddon and irreconcilable conflict between significant religious-cultural sectors of the world's population.

The beneficent function of religion in its truest form can never be doubted, for in the words of Whitehead, in defining its function, "religion is force of belief cleansing the inward parts."[107] Therefore, Deists may be members or active supporters of any church they choose on the grounds that it acts not only as a socially desirable bonding institution but also seeks to promote practical good for humanity on a global scale, providing they refrain from subscribing to its theological doctrines as constituting real truths.

Many things have been stated in this book which will startle churchmen of all faiths everywhere. This has not so much been inevitable as intentional, for how else can a world ecumenicalism of all major faiths be achieved with honesty without first undergoing the catharsis of self-criticism? Understanding our neighbour must be the first duty of the churchman in today's global village, and the huge diversity of cultures necessitates that such understanding cannot hope to be achieved without attempting to throw off all those notions planted in our minds through nurture and education.

Those statements that might seem to startle the settled minds of churchmen and churchwomen have been proffered as issues for discussion, since they concern matters which refuse to vanish. If the main thrust of this book, which is an appeal for a new objective idealism in creating a practical ethical world consciousness through the power of deism, acts as a catalyst in bringing into fruition a world religious revival, then the highest hopes of the author will have been achieved.

****

---

[107] Whitehead, op. cit., p. 5.

APPENDIX

List of Works and their Authors published during the great era of English Deism between 1690-1740

In response to those scholars who have attempted to either underestimate or disparage the achievements and huge literary output of British deism as a significant intellectual movement in the first half of the 18th century, and shortly before, the following list is given of leading deists and their works during this period. The works are listed in approximate chronological order.

Ralph Cudworth (1617-1688) a Cambridge Platonist
> *The True Intellectual System of the Universe* (1678); *Treatise Concerning Eternal & Immutable Morality*, published posthumously in 1731

Charles Blount (1654-1693)
> *Anima Mundi* (1679); *Great is Diana of the Ephesians* (1680); *The Two First Books of Philostratus concerning the Life of Apollonius Tyaneus* (1680); *Summary Account of The Deist's Religion* (1693); *Miscellaneous Works*, with preface by Charles Gildon, 1695.

John Locke (1632-1704)
> *The Reasonableness of Christianity* (1695)

John Toland (1670-1722)
> *Christianity not mysterious: or a Treatise Shewing That there is nothing in the Gospel contrary to Reason, nor above it: And that no Christian Doctrine can properly be call'd a Mystery* (1696); *Letters to Serena* (1704) being a discussion of Spinoza's deism, a work dedicated to the Queen of Prussia, being the daughter of the Electress Sophia of Hanover; *Nazarenus; or Jewish, Gentile, & Mahometan Christianity* (1718), which despite being based on false scholarship is valuable for the remarkable reflections on the differences between the Jewish and Gentile Christians in the early church; and, *Pantheisticon, sive formula celebrandae sodalitatis Socraticae* (1720)

Thomas Woolston (1670-1731)

The Old Apology for the Truth of the Christian Religion against the Jews & Gentiles Revived (1705); *Discourse on the Miracles of Our Saviour, In view of The Present Contest between Infidels & Apostates* (1727-1729)

Anthony Collins (1676-1729)

An Essay concerning The Use of Reason in propositions the evidence whereof depends on Human Testimony (1707); *Priestcraft in Perfection* (1709); *Vindication of the Divine Attributes* (1710); *Discourse of Free-Thinking, occasioned by the Rise & Growth of a Sect called Free-thinkers* (1713); *Philosophical Inquiry concerning Human Liberty* (1715); *Discourse of the Grounds & Reasons of the Christian Religion* (1724); *Scheme of Literal Prophecy Considered* (1725); *Dissertation on Liberty & Necessity* (1729)

William Wallaston (1660-1724)

The Religion of Nature Delineated (1724)

Matthew Tindal (c1657-1733)

Christianity as Old as Creation: Or, The Gospel A Republication of the Religion of Nature (1730); *The Analogy of Religion* (1736)

Thomas Chubb (1679-1746)

The Supremacy of the Father asserted (1715); *A Discourse Concerning Reason, with Regard to Religion & Divine Revelation* (1731); *The True Gospel of Jesus Christ Asserted* (1732); *The True Gospel of Jesus Christ Vindicated* (1739); *An Enquiry Into The Ground & Foundation of Religion, wherein is shewn, that Religion is founded in Nature* (1740); *A Discourse on Miracles, Considered as Evidence to prove the Divine Original of a Revelation* (1741); *Posthumous Works* (1748)

Thomas Morgan (d. 1743)

The Moral Philosopher, being the first of a 3-volume work, Volume I: *In A Dialogue between Philalethes, a Christain Deist, & Theophanes, a Christian Jew* (1737); Volume II: *Being a farther Vindication of Moral Truth & Reason* (1739);

and, Volume III: *Superstition & Tyranny inconsistent with Theocracy* (1740)

Lord Bolingbroke (1678-1751)
Philosophical Works ed. by David Mallett in 1752

Peter Annet (1693-1769)
The Resurrection of Jesus examined by a Moral Philosopher (1744); *A Collection of Tracts of a certain Free Enquirer* (1739-45)

The above list of authors and cited works are those which are acknowledged as overtly deistic, but a fine line may be drawn between acknowledged deists and moralists of the same period, many of the latter being in holy orders, although engaged in philosophical rather than theological writings. Amongst the huge number of borderline deists of this period may be mentioned Conyers Middleton (1683-1750) author of the well-known book, *Free Enquiry into the Miraculous Powers which are supposed to have existed in the Christian Church through several successive Ages* (1748) which also highlights the pagan origins in much of Christian tradition; and the writings of Anthony Astley Cooper, third Earl of Shaftesbury (1671-1713).

BIBLIOGRAPHY

Note: The following bibliography concentrates on studies of deism and related topics from the mid-19th century onwards. Works published during the great age of English deism are listed in the Appendix. Other works on deism and related topics discussed in the main text will also be found in the Index if not listed below.

Abbey, C.J. & Overton, J.H., *The English Church in the 18th Century*, 2 vols., London, 1878.

Aldridge, Alfred O., "Shaftesbury & the Deist Manifesto," *Transactions of American Philosophical Society*, new ser., Vol. 41, Part 2 (1951), 297-385.

Alexander, Prof. Samuel, *Space, Time & Deity*, Gifford Lectures, 2 Vols., 1920.

Bar, James, *Biblical Faith & Natural Theology: The Gifford Lectures for 1991*, OUP, 1995.

Becker, Carl L., *The Heavenly City of the 18th-Century Philosophers*, New Haven, 1932.

Berlin, Isaiah, ed., *The Age of Enlightenment*, NY, 1956.

Betts, C.J., *Early Deism in France: From the so-called 'deistes' of Lyon (1564) to Voltaire's 'Lettres philosophiques' (1734)*, Martinus Nijhoff, 1884.

Boller, Paul F. jnr., *George Washington & Religion*, Dallas, Texas, 1963.

Bury, J.B.A., *A History of Freedom of Thought*, OUP, 1913.

Cassirer, Ernst, *The Philosophy of the Enlightenment*, Princeton, 1951.

Cole, G.D.H., *Richard Carlile*, London, 1943.

Colie, R.L., *Light & Enlightenment: A Study of the Cambridge Platonists & the Dutch Arminians*, Cambridge, 1957.

Copleston, Frederick, *History of Philosophy,* Burns & Oates, 1999 ed., 9 Vols.

Courtines, Leo P., *Bayle's Relations with England & the English*, NY, 1938.

Cragg, G.R., *From Puritanism to the Age of Reason*, Cambridge, 1950.

Craig, William Lane, *The Historical Argument for the Resurrection of Jesus During the Deist Controversy*, Edwin Mellen, 1985.

Creed, John M., & Smith, John S. Boys, eds., *Religious Thought in the 18th Century*, Cambridge, 1934.

Davies, P.C.W., *Mind of God: The Scientific Basis for a Rational World*, Touchstone Books, 1993.

BIBLIOGRAPHY

Dawes, Gregory W., "The Challenge of the 17th Century," in *The Historical Jesus Question*, Westminster: John Knox Press, 2001.

Dawkins, Richard, *The God Delusion*, Bantam Press, 2006.

Farrar, A.S., *Critical History of Free Thought*, London, 1862.

Frazer, Sir James, *The Golden Bough*, Macmillan, 1936 ed., 13 Vols.

Frazer, Sir James, *Totemism & Exogamy*, Macmillan, 1910, 4 Vols.

Gay, Peter, *Deism: An Anthology*, Van Nostrand, 1967.

Guizot, F.P.G., *Lectures on European Civilization*, John Macrone, 1837.

Gwatkin, H.M., *The Knowledge of God*, T. & T. Clarke, Edinburgh, 1931.

Hall, Thomas C., *The Religious Background to American Culture*, Boston, 1930.

Hampshire, Stuart, ed., *The Age of Reason: The 17th Century Philosophers*, NY, 1956.

Havens, George R., *The Age of Ideas*, NY, 1955.

Hazard, Paul, *European Thought in the 18th Century*, 1954.

Hazard, Paul, *La Crise de la conscience européenne*, 3 vols., Paris, 1935.

Hedges, Chris, *American Fascists: The Christian Right & The War on America*, Jonathan Cape, 2007.

Hefelbower, S.G., *The Relation of John Locke to English Deism*, Chicago, 1918.

Herrick, James A., *The Radical Rhetoric of the English Deists: The Discourse of Skepticism 1680-1750*, Univ. of South Carolina Press, 1997.

Humphreys, A.R., *The Augustan World*, London, 1954.

Hunt, John, *Religious Thought in England from the Reformation to the end Of the last Century*, 3 Vols., London, 1873.

Huxley, Julian, *Religion Without Revelation*, Max Parrish, 1957.

Janssen, Johannes, *History of the German People At The End of the Middle Ages*, Kegan, Praul, Trench, Trübner, & B. Herder, London & St. Louis, 1896-1910, 16 Vols.

Jordan, Wilbur K., *Development of Religious Toleration in Englnd*, Cambridge, Mass., 1932-40, 4 Vols.

Koch, G. Adolf, *Republican Religion: The American Revolution & the Cult of Reason*, NY, 1933.

Lecky, W.E.M., *History of the Rise & Influence of Rationalism in Europe*, Longmans Green, London, 1865, 2 Vols.

Leland, John, *A View of the Principal Deistical Writers that have appeared In England in the last & present Century*, 3rd, ed., London, 1754.56, 3 Vols.

Lovejoy, A.O., "The Parellal of Deism & Classicism," *Modern Philology*, Vol. XXIX (1932), 281-299.

Luke, Hugh J. jnr., *Drams for the Vulgar: A Study of Some Radical Publishers & Publications of Early 19th Century London*,

Unpublished Ph.D dissertation, Univ. of Texas, 1963.

Marais, Herbert M., *Deism in 18th Century America*, NY, 1934.

Martin, Kingsley, *French Liberal Thought in the 18th Century*, Boston, 1929.

McIntyre, Alasdair, *A Short History of Ethics*, Routledge & Kegan Paul, 1967.

McKee, David Rice, *Simon Tyssot de Patot & the 17th Century Background of Critical Deism*, John Hopkins Press, 1941.

Mead, Margaret, *Male & Female*, Gollancz, 1949.

Mencken, H.L., *Treatise On Right & Wrong*, Paul, Trench, Trübner, 1934.

Metchnikov, Ilya, *The Nature of Man*, NY, 1903.

M'Giffert, Arthur C., *Protestant Thought Before Kant*, London, 1919.

Moltmann-Wendel, Dr. Elisabeth, *Ein eigener Mensch warden: Frauen um Jesus*, Gütersloher Verlagshaus, 4th ed., 1984.

Mossner, Ernest C., *Bishop Butler & the Age of Reason*, NY, 1936.

Orr, John, *English Deism: Its Roots & Its Fruits*, Eerdmans, 1934.

Osler, Sir William, *Science & Immortality*, Boston, 1904.

Pagel, Elaine, *Gnostic Gospels*, Penguin Books.

Parrington, Vernon L., *Main Currents in American Thought*, NY, 1927, 3 Vols.

Pascal, Blaise, *Thoughts*, Geroge Bell, Bohn's Standard Library ed., 1890.

Popkin, Richard H., "Scepticism in the Enlightenment," *Studies on Voltaire & the 18th Century*, Geneva, XXIV/XXVII (1963), 1321-1345.

Rawls, John, *A Theory of Justice*, OUP, 1970.

Renan, Ernest, *Life of Jesus*, Everyman ed., 1927.

Rinaldo, Peter M., *Atheists, Agnostics, & Deists in America: A Brief History*, Dorpete, Pv., 2000.

Robertson, *A Short History of Freethought Ancient & Modern*, Watts & Co., 1906 ed., 2 Vols.

Robinson, John, *Honest To God*, SCM, 1963.

Russell, Bertrand, *History of Western Philosophy*, Allen & Unwin, 1946.

Russell, Bertrand, *Human Society In Ethics & Politics*, Allen & Unwin, 1954.

Salvatorelli, Luigi, *From Locke to Reitzenstein: the Historical Investigation of the Origins of Christianity*, Cambridge, Mass., 1930.

Sargant, William, *Battle For The Mind*, Heinemann, 1952.

Sayous, Edouard, *Les Déistes anglais et le christianisme, 1696-1738*, Paris, 1882.

Schopenhauer, Arthur, *Essays*, Allen & Unwin, 1951.

Seeley, J.R., *Ecce Homo*, Macmillan, Eversley ed., 1903.

Sidgwick, Henry, *Outlines of The History of Ethics*, Macmillan, 6th ed., 1931.

Stephen, Leslie, *English Thought in the 18th Century*, London, 1876, 2 Vols.

Stromberg, Roland, N., *Religious Liberalism in 18th Century England*, Oxford, 1954.

Tawney, R.H. *Religion & The Rise of Capitalism*, John Murray, 1926.

Tennant, F.R., *Miracle & Its Philosophical Presuppositions*, Cambridge, 1925.

Thouless, R.H., *An Introduction To The Psychology of Religion*, Cambridge, 1923.

Torrey, Norman, L., ed., *Les Philosophes*, NY, 1960.

Torrey, Norman, L., *Voltaire & the English Deists*, New Haven, 1930.

Tulloch, John, *Rational Theology & Christian Philosophy in England in the 17th Century*, Edinburgh & London, 1872.

Waring, E. Graham, *Deism & Natural Religion: A Source Book*, 1967.

Walters, Kerry, *The American Deists: Voices of Reason & Dissent in the Early Republic*, Univ. Press of Kansas, 1992.

Webb, Clement C.J., *Studies in the History of Natural Theology*, Oxford, 1915.

Weber, Max, *The Protestant Ethic & The Spirit of Capitalism*, trans. by Talcott Parsons, Charles Scribner, NY, 1958.

Wheless, Joseph, *Is It God's Word?*, A. Knopf, NY, 1936.

Whitehead, A.N., *Religion In The Making*, Lowell Lectures, Cambridge UP, 1927.

Whyte, Adam Gowans, *The Religion of The Open Mind*, Watts & Co., 1913.

Willey, Basil, *The 18th Century Background*, 1940.

Winnett, A.R., "Were the Deists 'Deists?'", *Church Quarterly Review*, Vol. CLXI (1960), 70-77.

Wolterstorff, Nicholas, *Reason Within The Bounds of Religion*, Eerdmans, 1984.

Yolton, John W., *John Locke & the Way of Ideas*, Oxford, 1956.

USEFUL WEBSITES

World Union of Deists:- www.deism.com
Deist Alliance:- www.deistalliance.org/
The Deist Net:- www.deistnet.com/
Dynamic Deism:- www.dynamicdeism.org/
Deist Information:- www.deist.info/
Modern Deism:- www.moderndeism.com/
History of Deism:- www.wikipedia.org/wiki/Deism
DeismNewsGroup:-www.alt.religion.deism

INDEX

LaVergne, TN USA
07 October 2010
199900LV00001B/136/A

9 780954 316198